COMPUTING MADE EASY

FOR THE OVER 50s

SUITABLE FOR WINDOWS VISTA

First published in the UK in 2009 by Which? Books
Which? Books are commissioned and published by Which? Ltd, 2 Marylebone Road, London NW1 4DF
Email: books@which.co.uk

British Library Cataloguing in Publication Data
A catalogue record for this book is available from the British Library

ISBN 978 1 84490 068 8

7 9 10 8

The publishers would like to thank Sarah Kidner and the Which? Computing team for their help in the preparation of
this book.

Consultant Editor: Terrie Chilvers
Project Manager: Kirstie Addis
Designer: Blanche Williams, Harper-Williams
Proofreader: Chris Turner
Indexer: Lynda Swindells
Printed and bound by: Charterhouse, Hatfield
Distributed by Littlehampton Book Services Ltd, Faraday Close, Durrington, Worthing, West Sussex BN13 3RB

Essential Silk is an elemental chlorine-free paper produced at Condát in Perigord, France, using timber from
sustainably managed forests. The mill is ISO14001 and EMAS certified.

For a full list of Which? Books, please call 01903 828557, go to www.which.co.uk, or write to Littlehampton Book
Services. For other enquiries, call 0800 252 100.

COMPUTING
MADE
EASY

SUITABLE FOR
WINDOWS
VISTA

FOR THE OVER 50s

Contents

▶ STAYING IN TOUCH

▶ MEDIA & CREATIVITY

▶ MAINTAIN YOUR PC

▶ SECURITY

▶ TROUBLESHOOTING

▶ JARGON BUSTER

INTRODUCTION

Using a computer needn't be a stressful experience. With this book you can get to grips with your PC and find out how to get the most out of it. From basic tasks such as how to save a document to fun activities like sharing your photos or listening to music, you'll find step-by-step instructions and advice that's easy to understand.

Computing Made Easy is designed to guide you through everything you need to know to become a competent computer user. Once you've found your way around your computer in the early chapters and mastered the basics, you can move on to other topics such as using the internet, emailing or chatting online via a webcam. Later chapters will show you how to manage your photos, music and video footage, as well as how to keep your computer secure and in good working order, plus lots more.

You can either work through the book chapter by chapter, dip into a specific chapter, or use the Contents page or Index if you want to find advice on a particular subject.

There's no time like the present – turn on your computer and let's get started.

EDITORIAL NOTE

The instructions in this guide refer to the Windows Vista operating system. Where other software or websites are mentioned, instructions refer to the latest versions (at the time of going to print). If you have a different version, the steps may vary slightly.

Screenshots are used for illustrative purposes only.

Windows Vista is an American product. All spellings on the screenshots and on the buttons and boxes in the text are therefore spelled in US English. The rest of the text remains in UK English.

All technical words in the book are either discussed in jargon busters within the text and/or can be found in the Jargon Buster section on page 213.

GETTING STARTED

By reading and following all the steps in this chapter, you will get to grips with:

▷ **Finding your way around your PC**

▷ **Using the keyboard and mouse**

▷ **Understanding Windows**

▶ The Basics

GET TO KNOW YOUR PC

Whether you've just bought a new PC or want to get to know your current one better, here is a list of the most important features. Often these are within the computer 'tower' – the lines are a guide only.

DISC DRIVES
Most computers contain a CD/DVD drive to play discs and, in some cases, a DVD-RW drive that allows you both to play disks and record (burn) onto them – check for the RW logo on the drive. If not, there's the option to buy a separate, external DVD writer.

MEMORY
Your computer's short-term memory, or Ram, determines how many programs can run at the same time. Depending on what you'll use it for (video-editing, for example, uses more memory than word processing software), 2GB Ram is OK for an average user.

MONITOR
Modern PCs come with a flat panel monitor.

OPERATING SYSTEM
The software that runs your computer. PCs now come with Windows Vista or Windows 7. There are four versions of Vista – Home Basic, Home Premium, Business and Ultimate – each with a slightly different set of features. Most people will be best served with Home Premium, which is aimed at those who want to use their PC for a bit of everything.

PROCESSOR
Also known as the Central processing unit (CPU), this is the engine of your computer and determines its speed (in GHz/gigahertz). A 2GHz processor should suit average users. Processors are made by either Intel or AMD. Most CPUs are now dual core (they have two processors on one chip that share the workload). Quad-core technology is also available.

HARD DISK DRIVE
Where your computer stores all your software and files. The size is measured in gigabytes (GB). Most desktop PCs come with 300GB or more, which should be plenty – but bear in mind what you'll be using your computer for. Storing videos, lots of music, high-resolution photos and installing games uses up space quickly. If in doubt, always go for more space.

GRAPHICS CARD
Responsible for displaying images on your computer. Integrated graphics mean the graphics share the computer's Ram (memory), which often makes the computer slower. If you plan to play games, edit videos or watch films you should choose a PC with a good graphics card with its own Ram so it can perform well without drawing on your computer's memory.

MOUSE
Used to move your cursor around the screen. There are two main types: ball and optical. Optical mice operate by emitting a light from an LED or laser, while ball mice rely on a mechanical system of rollers and an internal ball. A mouse can be wireless or connected with a USB or firewire cable.

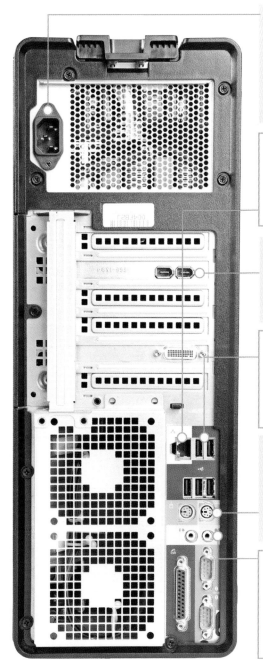

POWER SUPPLY
Plug your PC's power supply cable in here. Your computer may also have an on/off switch at the back (although you will rarely need to use this). To turn your PC on, use the button at the front.

ETHERNET PORT
Sometimes called the network port, this lets you connect computers over a network or plug in a modem or router.

FIREWIRE PORTS
Firewire cables transfer data to and from digital devices such as digital camcorders and MP3 players.

USB PORTS
Many devices such as printers and scanners connect via USB ports. You may also have a USB port on the side of your monitor.

KEYBOARD AND MOUSE PORTS
Ports for the keyboard and mouse are often colour-coded, or will have an icon next to them. Newer devices may connect via USB.

SPEAKERS AND HEADPHONES
Sockets where you can plug in sound devices. They're often colour-coded with icons to help you plug into the right one.

TIP
You can add extra storage to your existing PC by investing in an external hard drive. See page 185.

Jargon buster

Software
A general term for programs used to operate computers and related devices.

NEXT STEP

Once you've set up your computer, you'll want to get online. See page 68 for how to get connected.

⏵ The Basics

YOUR DESKTOP EXPLAINED

The desktop is the screen you see as soon as you start up Windows. Here, you'll find icons linking to documents, programs or specific areas of your computer. One key area is the desktop itself: this is a good place to save projects that you're currently working on for easy access. Our top tips on page 22 will show you how to customise it.

DESKTOP ICONS
Shortcuts to specific programs, documents or areas of your computer. Simply double click on these icons.

QUICK LAUNCH BAR
An area within Windows, which displays shortcuts to your favourite programs.

VISTA ICON
Provides a quick way to perform many common tasks, such as launching programs or opening menus, such as the Control Panel.

DOCUMENT/PROGRAM BUTTONS
Any documents and programs you have minimised
(see page 16) will
appear here.

DESKTOP
A computer display area that represents the kinds
of objects you might find on a real desktop, such as
documents and project folders.

TASKBAR
Shows you which applications or tasks are active and
running. Some taskbars include icons for commonly used
programs.

THE MOUSE

The majority of computer mice feature two buttons and a scroll wheel. Here's how to get to grips with your mouse.

Single click Sometimes referred to as left-clicking; involves clicking the left-hand mouse button just once. Whenever you're instructed simply to click on something, this means a single left click.

Double click Clicking the left-hand mouse button twice in quick succession is known as double-clicking. You often need to double click on an icon to open a program, or on a document name to open a file.

Right click Pressing the right-hand button or right-clicking often reveals a list of functions you can perform (see left). Highlighting text and right-clicking within a Word document, for example, reveals options to change the appearance of a paragraph (see page 43 for more on formatting paragraphs).

Highlighting Click your mouse at the beginning of the paragraph and keep it held down. Drag your mouse cursor to the end of the paragraph or section of text and release the mouse button. Your selected text will be highlighted and you can either right click to access further actions, or use the toolbar at the top of your screen to make changes.

Drag and drop Mostly used to move objects or documents from one place to another. For example, to move a file from one folder to another, click once with your left-hand mouse button to select the object, keep the button depressed and drag the object towards its new folder. The file will move with the cursor; let go of the mouse button to drop the file into its new location.

Scrolling Most mice have a scroll wheel between the left- and right-hand mouse buttons. To scroll down, click on the page once and roll the scroll wheel towards you. Alternatively, press down on the scroll wheel once and move the mouse back and forth to move down or up a page. If your mouse doesn't have a scroll wheel, click on the up or down arrow on the right-hand side of any page, or drag the bar between the arrows if it's a long document or web page.

TRY THIS

Often hovering your cursor over something will reveal another menu without the need to click on anything at all.

THE KEYBOARD

SHIFT KEY
Pressing the Shift key in combination with other keys performs a variety of different functions.

FUNCTION KEYS
Perform specific tasks depending on which program you're using. For example, pressing F5 in Microsoft Word will bring up a box that allows you to search for a specific word in your document. Pressing F5 when you're using the internet will reload (refresh) the web page you're looking at.

CTRL KEY
Like the Shift key, this key is used in combination with others to perform certain functions.

THE WINDOWS KEY
Pressing this key will open up the main Vista menu.

ENTER
Also known as the Return key. You can often use this key once you've submitted information (on an online form, for example) and want to progress to the next step. It will also start a new line on a Word document.

Selecting files Click with your mouse on a single file to select it. If you want to select a number of files at once – for example, to delete multiple files or attach various documents to an email – press and hold the Shift key and click on the top and bottom files in the list to select all the files in the list. Alternatively, you can select odd files (every other file, say). Hold down the Ctrl key and click with your mouse on every file that you wish to select.

Copy and paste To copy a section of text or an image, press **Ctrl** and hold while you also press **C**. Then find the location you want to copy it to, press **Ctrl** and hold while pressing **V**. This is useful if you want to copy information on a web page, for example, into a Word document or email. If you want to cut text completely from one document and paste in another, press **Ctrl** and hold while pressing **X**. Then paste as above. Pressing **Ctrl** and **Z** will undo the last task you performed (for example, if you delete a whole paragraph by mistake and want to get it back).

NAVIGATION KEYS
Allow you to move around in documents or web pages. Most do what they say. Pressing the Home key will take you to the start of a line if you're using word processing software; the End key will take you to the end of a line. The Insert key forces any text you type to overwrite what's already there.

NEXT STEP ▶

Learn more keyboard shortcuts in the Creating Documents chapter on page 52.

OPEN A PROGRAM

Once you've turned on your computer, the next step is to open a program. For example, you might want to open Microsoft Word to write a letter, or Internet Explorer to surf the internet.

There are two ways to do this. You can:

1 Double click on an icon on the desktop

2 The program will open in a new window

or:

1 Click 🪟

2 Select what you want to open from the list, for example, Email, Internet Explorer, Windows Media Player or Photo Gallery

TRY THIS

You can rearrange the icons on your desktop by right-clicking on a blank area, then clicking **Sort by**. You can choose to arrange them by name, size, type or date modified.

3 If you can't see the program you want, click on the Search box (titled **Start Search**) and type it in. A list of options will appear as you type

4 Click on the one you want and it will open in a new window

CREATE A SHORTCUT

When you use Vista for the first time, you will already have icons on the desktop to make it quick and easy to get straight into common programs. To add a desktop shortcut for another program:

1 Right click on a blank part of the desktop

2 In the menu that appears, hover your cursor over **New**. A second menu will appear

3 Click **Shortcut**

4 Click **Browse** and select the program you want to create a shortcut for. Click **OK**

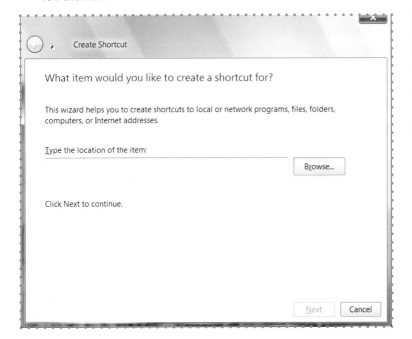

Jargon buster

Icon
A small picture that represents an object or program.

5 Click **Next**

6 Type a name for your shortcut – this can be the name of the program or your own made-up name

7 Click **Finish**

TIP
If you delete a shortcut, you're not deleting the program itself, just the shortcut.

HANDLING WINDOWS

When you open a program or a web page, it will open as a window on your desktop. You can adapt these windows to the size you want and have more than one available to you at the same time.

CROSS ICON
This will close the window and you'll have to open the program afresh if you want to use it again. Depending on which program you're using you may see two crosses – one for the file you're working on and one for the program as a whole. For example, in Microsoft Word, you will have the option to close either the document or Word completely.

MINIMISE ICON
Click and the window will disappear from the desktop and appear as a button on the taskbar (see page 18). Click on the corresponding taskbar button and the window will reappear.

MAXIMISE ICON
Click and the window will occupy the whole of the screen. Click again and your window will return to its original size.

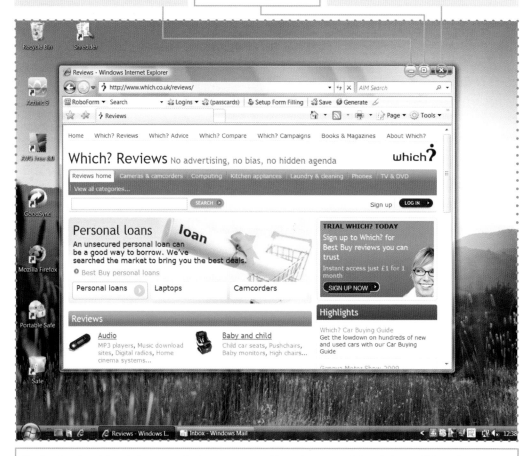

To alter the size of the window manually, hover near one side or the corner of the window until the pointer changes into a double-headed arrow, ◄─► click and drag the border up, down, across or diagonally, to the size you want.

Main Menus

The Main Menu is generally the toolbar at the top of the screen. A toolbar is a row, column or block of buttons or icons representing tasks you can do within a program.

When you click on the words or tabs at the top of the screen they will open to reveal further options. Click on **Page Layout** in Microsoft Word, for instance, and you'll see options such as adding columns or altering the size of margins.

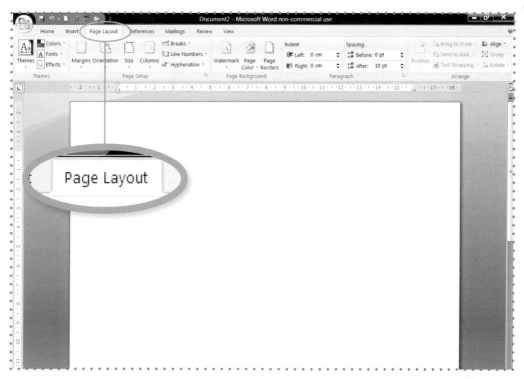

NEXT STEP

To learn more about the taskbar at the bottom of the screen, see page 18.

THE TASKBAR

The taskbar is the bar that sits at the bottom of your desktop from where you can access the main Windows functions. You can open a number of programs at any one time and switch between them by clicking on the taskbar. When you minimise a window it can also be reinstated at any time by clicking on it in the taskbar. You may not see the full title of each program/window in the taskbar as they are shrunk down to fit. If you're unsure what you want, hover your cursor over each and the full title will appear.

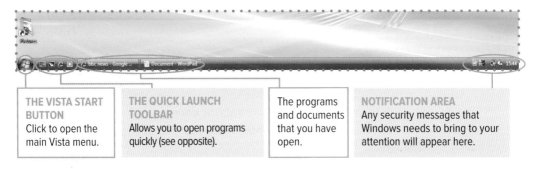

THE VISTA START BUTTON
Click to open the main Vista menu.

THE QUICK LAUNCH TOOLBAR
Allows you to open programs quickly (see opposite).

The programs and documents that you have open.

NOTIFICATION AREA
Any security messages that Windows needs to bring to your attention will appear here.

Resize the taskbar

TIP
You can close a program by right-clicking on it in the taskbar and clicking **Close**.

1. Right click on an empty space on the taskbar

2. A small window will appear. If **Lock the Taskbar** has a tick mark next to it, the taskbar is locked

3. Unlock it by clicking **Lock the Taskbar**. This will remove the tick.

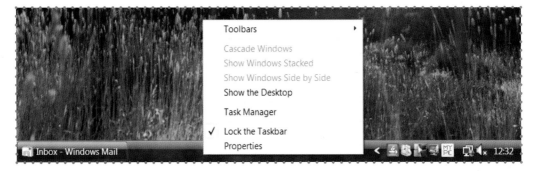

4. Hover your cursor over the edge of the taskbar until it changes into a double-headed arrow and drag the border up, or down

USE THE QUICK LAUNCH TOOLBAR

To get easy access to programs that you use often, add them to the Quick Launch toolbar on your taskbar.

1 Right click an empty area of the taskbar and hover over **Toolbars**. Another menu will appear

2 Select **Quick Launch**. The Quick Launch toolbar will appear on your taskbar

3 Find the icon of a program you want to add (either from the desktop or Vista Start menu – see page 14) and drag it to the Quick Launch toolbar

4 Now (and in the future) open the program by clicking on the icon in the toolbar

5 To remove the Quick Launch toolbar, right click and hover over **Toolbars** as in step 1, then click on **Quick Launch** again

Jargon buster

Toolbar
A vertical or horizontal onscreen bar that's made up of small images; click these to perform commands.

Jargon buster

Taskbar
The bar running across the bottom of your screen from where you can open programs and access the main Windows functions.

finding your way around

TIP
Hover over a program or document in the taskbar and you'll see a mini version of the page.

THE CONTROL PANEL

From the Control Panel you can make changes to your computer, including the appearance of your desktop, your security settings and the programs that are on your computer.

TIP
Can't find what you want in the Control Panel? Type it into the search box and let Vista find it.

To access the Control Panel:

1 Click

2 Click **Control Panel**. Click on one of the following headings for more options

3 Click on heading for more options

SYSTEM AND MAINTENANCE
View your computer's details and carry out tasks such as transferring or backing up your files.

SECURITY
Check your computer's security status and see if any security updates are available. For more on security see page 198.

NETWORK AND INTERNET
Set up an internet connection, connect to a network and repair problems with your existing connection (see pages 66-81 for more on this).

PROGRAMS
Uninstall any unwanted programs. Plus choose which program starts up automatically when you turn your computer on.

USER ACCOUNTS AND FAMILY SAFETY
Manage user accounts and set up parental controls. See page 94 for more details.

APPEARANCE AND PERSONALIZATION
Customise the appearance of your desktop and windows.

EASE OF ACCESS
Alter settings and access tools that make it easier to use your computer. For example, change the size of your text or alter the appearance of the mouse cursor. For more see page 23.

TURN YOUR COMPUTER OFF

When you've finished, there are options for switching your computer off.

 Puts your computer into 'sleep mode'. This saves your session and sends your computer into a low power state so that you can resume working from where you left off. Your screen will turn black; as soon as you press the On button (on the front of your computer), your computer will turn back on.

 Locks your computer. When you want to return to your session, you'll need to put in your password to resume.

To see all of Vista's other shutdown options, click

Switch user If somebody else wants to use the computer and has a user account, this will close your account and allow them to log on.

Log off This will close your session and take you back to the log-in screen.

Lock The same as clicking the padlock icon, as above.

Restart Your computer will switch off and immediately start up again. You may have to do this after installing software.

Sleep The same as clicking the 'sleep mode' icon, as above.

Shut down Your computer will switch off fully.

BE CAREFUL

Always shut down properly. Turning off your computer using only the On/Off button can cause problems the next time you start up.

NEXT STEP

For advice on PC security see page 198.

finding your way around

21

Customising your PC

PERSONALISE YOUR DESKTOP

You might want to change the appearance of your screen to make it more personal or easier to read:

COLOUR
Click on **Window Color and Appearance** and you can choose the colour of your windows, the Vista Start menu and taskbar.

1 Right click anywhere on the desktop

2 From the menu, click **Personalize**

3 Choose one of the following options to change how your screen looks

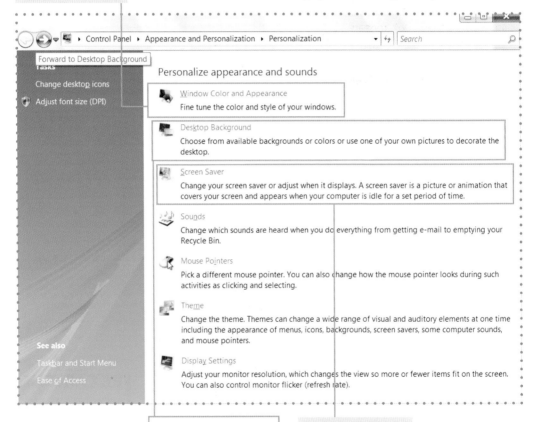

Control Panel ▸ Appearance and Personalization ▸ Personalization

Search

Forward to Desktop Background

Tasks
Change desktop icons
Adjust font size (DPI)

Personalize appearance and sounds

Window Color and Appearance
Fine tune the color and style of your windows.

Desktop Background
Choose from available backgrounds or colors or use one of your own pictures to decorate the desktop.

Screen Saver
Change your screen saver or adjust when it displays. A screen saver is a picture or animation that covers your screen and appears when your computer is idle for a set period of time.

Sounds
Change which sounds are heard when you do everything from getting e-mail to emptying your Recycle Bin.

Mouse Pointers
Pick a different mouse pointer. You can also change how the mouse pointer looks during such activities as clicking and selecting.

Theme
Change the theme. Themes can change a wide range of visual and auditory elements at one time including the appearance of menus, icons, backgrounds, screen savers, some computer sounds, and mouse pointers.

Display Settings
Adjust your monitor resolution, which changes the view so more or fewer items fit on the screen. You can also control monitor flicker (refresh rate).

See also
Taskbar and Start Menu
Ease of Access

DESKTOP BACKGROUND
Choose a picture to appear as your screen background, whether it appears as one large image, as a repeated image or whether it has a border.

SCREEN SAVER
Choose the image/animation that appears when your computer isn't being used and how quickly it starts up when you take a break from your computer.

NEXT STEP ▸

You can create a screen saver with your own photos. See page 24 to find out how.

Ease of Access Center

Windows Vista has an Ease of Access Center, from where you can tweak or customise your settings. To launch this, click **Control Panel** and then select **Ease of Access** and click on **Ease of Access Center**. Here are some tips on making your PC easier to use.

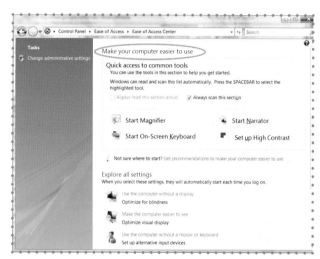

▶ **Make reading easier**

Click **Make the computer easier to see**. Scroll down and click **Change the size of text and icons**. If a warning box appears (related to your user account) click **Continue**. In the box called **DPI Scaling** select **Larger Scale (120 DPI) – make text more readable**, then click **OK** and restart your computer (see page 21).

▶ **Adjust mouse settings**

Click **Make the mouse easier to use**. Under the heading **Mouse pointers**, select the type of pointer you prefer from those shown. For example, you can make it bigger or a different colour. Click **Apply**.

TIP

To find out more about your keyboard, see page 13.

▶ **Magnify images and text**

The Magnifier is a virtual magnifying glass and is helpful for tasks including typing documents or reading a news story online. Click **Start Magnifier** and the top section of the screen will magnify the area over which you hover your cursor. You can adjust certain settings including scale of magnification and the location of the magnified content. Keep the box next to **Follow Mouse Cursor** ticked and the magnifier will enlarge the area around your mouse pointer. Close the **Magnifier** window to exit.

▶ **StickyKeys**

This tool bypasses the need to press several keys simultaneously when performing functions (such as **Ctrl + Alt + Delete** to switch users – see page 30). Instead, you'll only need to press one key at a time. Click **Make the keyboard easier to use** and tick the box next to **Turn on StickyKeys**.

Customising your PC

CREATE YOUR OWN SCREEN SAVER

Vista's Photo Gallery helps you create a screen saver with your photos. You'll need to add pictures to the Photo Gallery, then you can choose a screen saver using tags (descriptions of your images) or ratings to select your favourite images, or a combination of both.

1 Click

2 Click **All Programs** and select **Windows Photo Gallery**. This will display the images stored in the Pictures folder on your computer

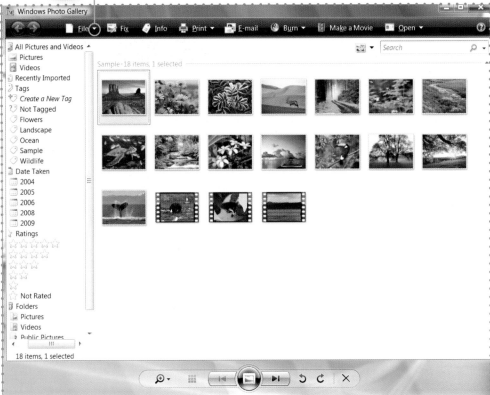

TRY THIS

If you don't want your slideshow to include all of your photos, click **Settings** in Step 4 and select **Use pictures and video from**. Choose the folder of pictures you'd like to use.

3 To use all the images in your Pictures folder, click the arrow next to **File**, and select **Screen Saver Settings** from the menu

④ From the drop-down menu select **Photos**

⑤ Click **Preview** to see what your new screen saver will look like – all your images will be displayed in sequence

⑥ You can adjust the length of time your computer will be inactive before your screen saver activates by selecting a time in the **Wait** box

⑦ A screen saver will be deactivated when you use the keyboard or move the mouse. Tick the **On Resume** box if you want to make sure that your password must be entered to access the computer at that point

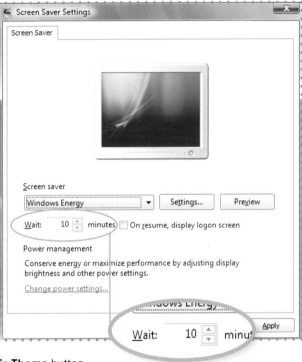

⑧ To customise your screen saver further, click on **Settings**. Adjust the speed of the screen saver, and choose the way that it displays the images by clicking on the **Use This Theme** button

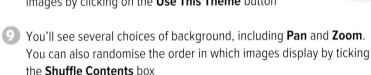

⑨ You'll see several choices of background, including **Pan** and **Zoom**. You can also randomise the order in which images display by ticking the **Shuffle Contents** box

BE CAREFUL

You can download screen savers from the internet, but watch out. Some may contain viruses or seriously slow down your computer. Only download from reputable sources.

Find out how to organise your photos on page 152.

ADD A SIDEBAR AND GADGETS

The sidebar is an area of the desktop that runs (by default) along the right-hand edge of the screen and plays host to your gadgets – mini applications that run on your desktop at all times. These gadgets provide instant access to useful things like a clock or calculator, as well as fun stuff like a mini slideshow of your photos.

If you can't see the sidebar, to open it:

1 Click ⊞

2 Click **All Programs**

3 Click **Accessories**

4 Click **Windows Sidebar**

To close it:

1 Right click on the sidebar

2 Click **Close Sidebar**

TIP

If you want the sidebar back, right click on the Sidebar icon in your taskbar then click **Open**.

> ▷ 📠 🖋 🗑 ⬆ 🖥 💿 📋   🖥 🔊ₓ 16:30

To add a gadget

1 Right click on the sidebar

2 Click **Add gadgets**

3 You'll see a list of gadgets you can choose from. Double click on a gadget to add it

To uninstall a gadget

1 Click the plus sign to open the Gadget Gallery

2 Right click on the gadget you no longer want and click **Uninstall**

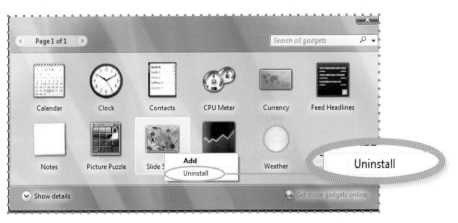

CREATE DIFFERENT USER ACCOUNTS

When you first set up your computer, Windows creates an Administrator account. This is an access-all-areas pass to your computer. Someone logged in on this account can install programs and make changes to the computer. If everyone who uses your computer has this level of access, it can cause problems. Plus, if you use this account as standard, it leaves you more open to security breaches.

Restricted user accounts – known as Standard accounts in Windows Vista – grant limited access to the computer (useful for younger members of the family). When you log into your user account, Windows knows which folders or files you may open, how you like your screen to look and what changes you're permitted to make to the computer. If you try to make a change you're not permitted to make, you'll be asked for the Administrator password.

TIP
To make changes to your user account click **Control Panel**, then **User Accounts** and select your account.

To create separate user accounts on your PC:

1 Click

2 Click on **Control Panel**, select **User Accounts and Family Safety**, then **Add or remove user accounts**

3 Click on **Create a new account**. Type in the user's name and select **Standard User**

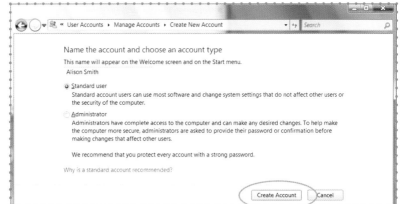

4 Click **Create Account**

5 A screen will come up with different accounts on it. Click on your new account and then click **Create a password**

6 You can change the picture icon that's allocated to each user account by selecting an image and then **Change the picture**

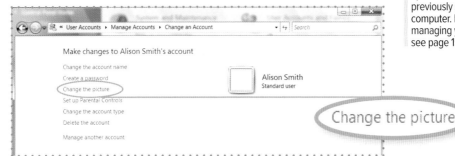

TRY THIS

You can use your own picture for your picture icon. Click on **Browse** when presented with the picture choices (in step 6) and select one you've previously saved on your computer. For more on managing your pictures see page 152.

7 If you want to limit how someone uses your computer, click **Set up Parental Controls** and select the account you want to restrict. Under **Windows Settings**, select what you'd like to control – for example, you can block websites or limit the time your child spends on the computer

8 When you've made your choices, select **On, enforce current settings**. Click **OK**

Customising your PC

SWITCH BETWEEN USERS

If you share a computer with someone else, you might need to switch to a different user while you're in the middle of using the PC.

1 Click

2 Click on the arrow icon

TIP

You can also switch users by pressing **Ctrl**, **Alt** + **Delete**, and selecting the account from the menu.

3 From the drop-down list, click **Switch user**. Your programs won't be closed down; when you switch back to your user account, everything will be as you left it

4 Select the user account you want to switch to

CREATING DOCUMENTS

By reading and following all the steps in this chapter, you will get to grips with:

 Using word processing software

 Formatting documents

 Creating a basic spreadsheet

OFFICE SUITES

An office suite is a package of programs that enables you to create, edit, read and manage a series of different documents. Generally, suites include a word processing and a spreadsheet program. They may also include a database program, presentation application, and a communication and personal organiser (email, calendar and contacts).

The software that came with your computer may contain a very basic word processor, such as Wordpad (that comes built into Windows), but investing in a proper office suite is something that almost every computer user should consider if they're going to make the most of their computer. Microsoft Office is one of several office suites available, and includes Microsoft Word and Microsoft Excel. Some other suites can even be downloaded for free, for example, OpenOffice at www.openoffice.org. This chapter covers Microsoft Word.

CREATE A DOCUMENT

To open a new word processing document on which to work:

TIP
To open an existing document, click **Open**.

1 Open Microsoft Word and click

2 From the drop-down list, select **New**

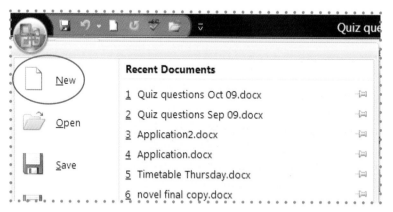

3 In the **New Document** window, click on the **Blank Document** icon

4 Click **Create** (bottom right). A new blank document will appear and you can begin typing

SAVE A DOCUMENT

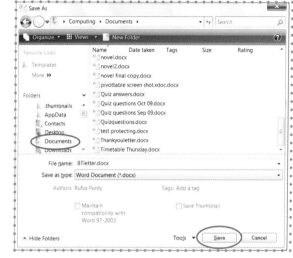

1 Click 🔲

2 From the drop-down list, select **Save**. If this is the first time you have saved your document, the **Save As** box will open

3 The default location for saving files is the Documents folder. Word will have given your document a name based on the first few words

4 Click **Save** if you're happy with these defaults

Alternatively, if you want to save your document somewhere different:

1 Browse to a different folder by using the shortcuts on the left-hand side of the **Save As** box

2 To name your document yourself click in the **File Name** box to highlight the name and type the name of your choice over the top of the default name

3 Click **Save**

Save as an older format

If someone you've sent a file to can't open it, it may be because they have an older version of Word (Word 2007 uses the .docx file format and this isn't always compatible with earlier versions). To ensure your documents can be opened and read using previous versions of Microsoft Word, first follow points 1 and 2 just above. Then:

1 Click the down arrow to the right of the box **Save as type**

2 Select Word 97 – 2003 Document from the drop-down list. This will create a .doc file

3 Click **Save**

TIP
Files will usually be saved to your hard drive by default – this will show up as your C: drive.

TRY THIS
If you try to close a document, without saving, don't worry – a dialogue box will prompt you to save it. Click **Yes** to save your document, **No** to lose any changes or **Cancel** to continue working on the document.

TRY THIS
You can also save your work by clicking the small **Save** icon just to the right of the Office button – it looks like a small floppy disk – or by pressing the **Ctrl** and then **S** keys on your keyboard.

Word

Word

THE WORD TOOLBAR

The main toolbar in Word is known as a ribbon. Key functions on this toolbar are organised under tabs.

The Home tab

Includes the basic formatting tools. From here, you can change the style, size and colour of your text, create bulleted and numbered lists and more. Find out how to use these on page 41.

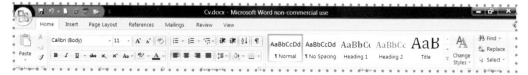

The Insert tab

Insert other elements into your document such as charts, shapes and pictures. You can also add headers and footers or the date and time. To find out how to add pictures to your document see page 45.

The Page Layout tab

Change the orientation of your page from vertical (Portrait – usually the default setting) to horizontal (Landscape), create multiple columns of text or add borders to your page (see page 54).

The References tab

A great tool for anyone writing long research documents or papers.
Insert endnotes and footnotes into long documents or create a table of
contents, and more.

The Review tab

Check the contents of your document using the spellchecker or
access the thesaurus. You can also use Track Changes, which is a way
of showing what changes you or others make to a single document.

The View tab

Zoom in or out of documents to make them easier to view. You can also see
how your document will look when printed out or published online.

NEXT STEP ⊙

Get to grips with
formatting documents
from page 41.

PRINT A DOCUMENT

Open your document (see page 32), then follow these steps to print out your work:

1 Click

2 In the drop-down list hover your mouse cursor over **Print**

3 Select **Quick Print**

To pick a different printer or print style:

1 Click

2 Click **Print**

3 To select a different printer – perhaps if one prints in black and white and another in colour – click the down arrow at the top of the screen and click on the relevant one

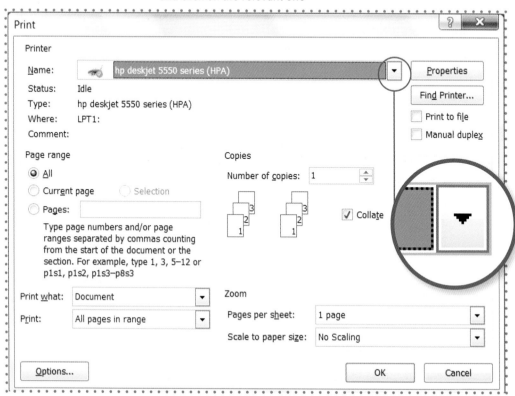

Print

Printer

Name: hp deskjet 5550 series (HPA)   Properties

Status: Idle   Find Printer...
Type: hp deskjet 5550 series (HPA)
Where: LPT1:   ☐ Print to file
Comment: ☐ Manual duplex

Page range   Copies
◉ All   Number of copies: 1
☐ Current page   ☐ Selection
☐ Pages: ☑ Collate
     Type page numbers and/or page
     ranges separated by commas counting
     from the start of the document or the
     section. For example, type 1, 3, 5–12 or
     p1s1, p1s2, p1s3–p8s3

Print what: Document   Zoom
Print: All pages in range   Pages per sheet: 1 page
                                   Scale to paper size: No Scaling

Options...   OK   Cancel

4 Click **OK** to print

5 To make changes to your printer's settings, click **Properties**. From here you can select which tray of the printer the paper should come from, change the size of paper you print on, or opt for double-sided printing if your printer has the capability. You can also choose the number of copies you want or print specific pages rather than the whole document.

Print Preview
If you want to see what your document will look like before you print:

1 Click [icon] and hover your mouse cursor over **Print**

2 Click **Print Preview**

3 Click the **Close Preview** button (top right) to return to your document and change it, or click **Print** (top left) if you're happy with it as it is

TIP
To go straight to the print menu, press
Ctrl + P.

NEXT STEP

For advice on connecting your printer, see page 81.

PRINT ERRORS EXPLAINED

Sometimes your document just doesn't print out as you want it to. Here are some of the more common printer errors you might come across.

Some of my text or images end up off the side of the printed page.
Start by checking the paper size option you're using. If you're using A4, click on the **Properties** button in the pop-up box that appears when you try to print. Make sure it's set to A4 and not US Letter. Click through the tabs in the **Properties** window and you may also see options for **Borderless Printing** or **Borderless Auto Fit**. Selecting one of these should ensure that nothing is cropped off by the margins. As a last resort, you may see an option in the main **Print** window – under **Zoom** – called **Scale to Paper Size** – set this to A4.

It's printing gibberish and spitting out paper. What's going wrong?
If this happens with all the documents that you try to print, you may need to reload or update the software that runs your printer.

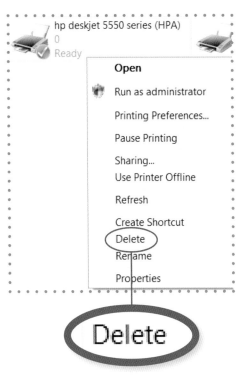

1. Disconnect your printer from the computer

2. Go to **Control Panel**

3. Click **Hardware and Sound**

4. Click **Printers**

5. Right click on the printer you're using

6. Select **Delete**

7. Click **Yes**

8. Visit your printer manufacturer's website and download the latest available driver for your printer, making sure you choose the version appropriate to your version of Windows (e.g. Windows XP or Windows Vista).

9. Follow the instructions to install and set up the software

I'm trying to print on both sides of the page to save on paper costs but the text is appearing upside down on the reverse of the paper.

How your printer handles double-sided printing will vary, and if it doesn't automate it in the printer (most don't), follow any onscreen instructions. Many printers have a helpful guide symbol inscribed on the paper tray, and you can use this to work out which way you need to insert the paper.

I want to print labels but they keep coming out wrong. Can you help?

Ensure you're using the right template. Avery makes industry standard labels that are supported by the templates in Microsoft Word and Outlook – you can download the templates from Office Online when you create a new document. Most Avery alternatives list the Avery number they correspond to. Pick a template that lists the Avery label (or equivalent) that you're using in your printer.

TIP

Save on paper by printing double-sided. This is often called duplex printing.

When I print a photo, the colours seem wrong or faded.

It's likely that your cartridges are running low or the ink nozzles are clogged. You'll need to print a test page:

1 Click

2 Click **Control Panel**

3 Click **Hardware and Sound**

4 Click **Printers**

5 Right click on the printer you're using

6 Select **Properties**

7 On the first tab, usually called **General**, click the **Print Test Page** button. The test page will show samples of black, cyan, magenta and yellow ink. If one of these is missing or faded, switch off and switch on the printer at the power source so that it resets and self-cleans

8 Repeat the test page. If you still have problems, you may need to replace your old printer cartridge (see your printer's instruction booklet)

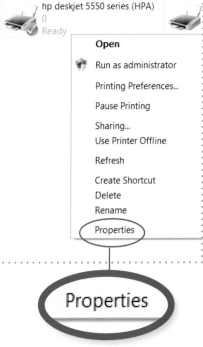

hp deskjet 5550 series (HPA)
0
Ready

Open
Run as administrator
Printing Preferences...
Pause Printing
Sharing...
Use Printer Offline
Refresh
Create Shortcut
Delete
Rename
Properties

Properties

My document won't print because another printing task (or job) is clogging up the print queue.

Your printer software organises jobs into a queue and, if one job fails, this can prevent any other work from being done. To check the print queue:

1 Click

2 Click **Control Panel**

3 Click **Hardware and Sound**. Double click on your printer

4 Click **Printers**

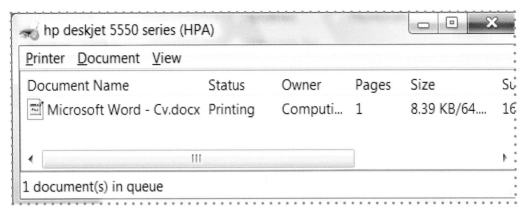

hp deskjet 5550 series (HPA)

Printer   Document   View

Document Name	Status	Owner	Pages	Size	Su
Microsoft Word - Cv.docx	Printing	Computi...	1	8.39 KB/64....	16

1 document(s) in queue

Jargon buster

Driver
Software that allows your computer to communicate with devices, such as a printer.

5 The **Status** column should tell you if a job has failed and why. To delete the job and get the queue moving again, click on the relevant document

6 Click **Document** in the top menu and then **Cancel** in the drop-down menu and restart your computer (see page 21)

I've replaced my ink cartridge but my printer isn't working.

Often the ink nozzles on the cartridge will initially be protected by a strip of tape. Check that you removed all of this when you put it in your printer.

NEXT STEP ▷

For more on drivers, see page 81.

Also, try switching the printer off and on again at the power source and disconnecting then reconnecting the USB lead that connects your computer and printer; your PC might not have recognised that you've changed a cartridge. Finally, see if any buttons are flashing on your printer. You may need to press the one that's flashing to get the printer online and back in action.

FORMAT A DOCUMENT

You can use Word's formatting tools to customise everything from the font, colour and size of individual text to the border of an image or the entire layout of your page. You can even apply new styles to whole documents at once and it's possible to preview what many of your changes will look like before you actually commit to them.

Many common formatting tasks can be carried out using the tools under the **Home** tab in the top toolbar. The Home tools are grouped under **Font**, **Paragraph**, **Styles** and **Editing**. In the **Font** segment of the toolbar, you'll find several options for changing the look, size and style of your text. In each case you'll need to highlight the text you want to change first by clicking next to it and dragging your mouse over it (see page 12).

SIMPLE TEXT FORMATTING

1 Highlight the text you want to alter

2 Click the down arrow next to the name of the current font in the toolbar to see a list of available fonts

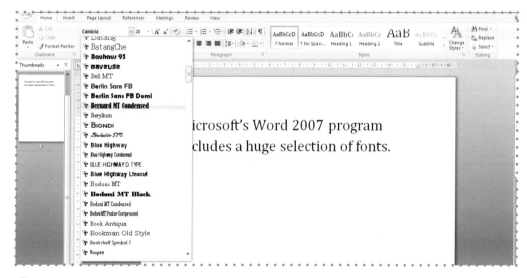

3 Scroll through the list and preview what the font will look like by hovering your mouse cursor over its name (without clicking). The highlighted text in your document will change for you to see what it would be like, but not permanently

④ To make the change, click on your chosen font's name in the list

⑤ Clicking the **B**, **I** or **U** buttons under **Font** in the toolbar will change the text you have highlighted to bold, italic or underlined respectively

⑥ You can increase the font size (and preview your changes) by clicking the down arrow next to the current font size (the default font size is 12)

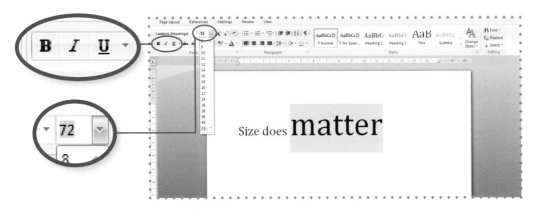

⑦ To change the colour of highlighted text, click the down arrow next to the **Font Colour** button (the one that features the letter 'A' underlined)

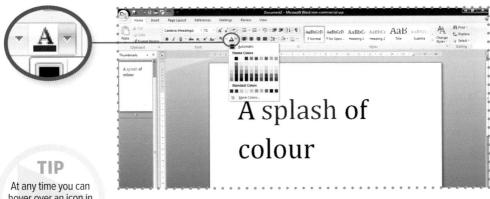

TIP

At any time you can hover over an icon in the main toolbar to reveal a description of what it does.

⑧ Hovering the mouse over a colour in the palette that appears will preview what your highlighted text will look like with that colour applied. Clicking on the colour will make the change

FORMAT PARAGRAPHS

With the Paragraph section of the Home tab, you can customise the layout of your page. Again, you'll need to highlight your text first (see page 12).

1 By default, Word aligns text to the left-hand side of the page. You can change this to centre your text, align to the right margin or alternatively justify your text in a block in the middle of your page.

2 To do this, select your text and click on one of the alternative alignment options just above where it says **Paragraph** in the **Home** toolbar

Jargon buster

Justified text
Justified text means that every line is spaced so that it's of equal length (flush with the right-hand margin).

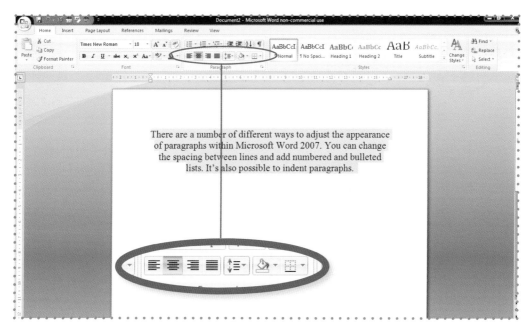

3 To change spacing between your lines, highlight your paragraph, right click and select **Paragraph**

4 Click the drop-down menu below **Line Spacing** and select from the various options. You can preview the effect by hovering over the option, before clicking to choose

5 Click **OK**

TRY THIS

You can create an indented paragraph by highlighting your paragraph and right-clicking. Select **Paragraph** and then, underneath the heading **Special**, select the drop-down arrow. Select **First line** from the list and click **OK**.

MAKE A BULLET-POINTED LIST

If you want to format any of your text in list form, you can use bullet point or numbering options.

1 Type your list into the document, pressing **Enter** on your keyboard after each item so that they are each on a separate line

2 Highlight your list and click on the down arrow on the bullet point button

3 In the drop-down menu that appears, preview the different bullet styles by holding your mouse cursor over them

4 Click to select your choice. The same principle applies to numbering your list with the numbering icon

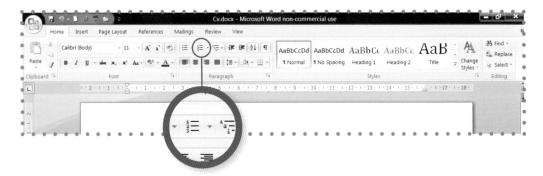

INSERT A PICTURE

1 Click once on the page at the point where you'd like the image to go

2 Click on the **Insert** tab on the top toolbar

3 Click the **Picture** icon

4 Look for the image you want and double click on it to insert it (for more on organising your pictures see page 152)

5 The toolbar across the top will change, showing a number of borders that you can apply to your photograph. Click on a border if you want one

6 In the **Arrange** part of the toolbar, you can change how the picture sits within the text. Highlight your image (click on it once) and click on the **Position** button. Hold your mouse over some of the options that appear to see where on your page your picture fits best. Click on the one that's best for you

Add a caption
You might want to add a caption to your picture:

1 Once it's in the document, right click on the picture and select **Insert Caption**

2 A dialogue box will appear. Enter your caption in the box marked **Caption**

3 Choose whether you want this to appear above or below your picture

4 Click **OK**

NEXT STEP

To find out more about editing your pictures, see page 154.

45

WORD TEMPLATES

Word comes with some useful templates and page layouts that you can use as the basis for a new document. To open a new document from one of Word's templates:

1 Click

2 Select **New**

3 In the left-hand column of the **New Document** dialogue box that appears, click on **Installed Templates**

4 Scroll through the installed templates that appear. To see a larger preview of a template in the right-hand column, click on it

5 Once you've chosen, click the template you want and then the **Create** button

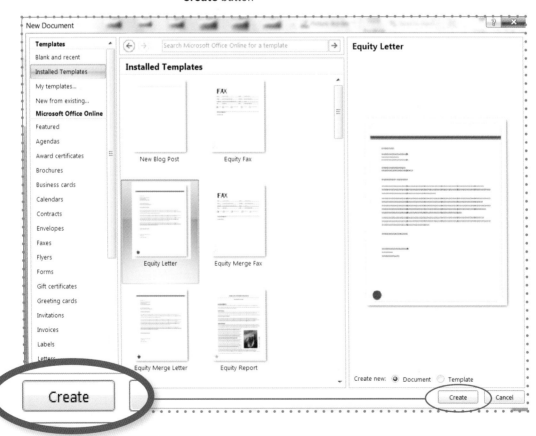

ONLINE TEMPLATES

You can also choose from a range of other templates from Microsoft Office Online (you'll need to be connected to the web – see page 68 for how to get online).

1 Follow the instructions to open a new Word template on the previous page, but, instead of clicking on Installed Templates in the New Document dialogue box, choose one of the subheadings under **Microsoft Office Online** in the left-hand column

2 Once the templates have loaded you can preview and select them as you would with a Word template (see opposite)

3 Click on **Create**. You may get a message that 'the status of your Microsoft Office' needs to be validated. This is simply a security measure to ensure you're using a genuine copy of Office

4 Click **Continue** and wait while your software is checked and the file downloads

SPELLCHECK A DOCUMENT

If there's a spelling error in your document, a wavy red line will appear under it (grammatical errors are underlined with a wavy green line).

1 Right click on the word

2 Select the correct version from the suggestions

TRY THIS

To turn off spellcheck, click the **Office** button, click **Word options**, then **Proofing**. Uncheck **When correcting spelling and grammar in Word.**

To spellcheck a whole document:

1 Click the **Review** tab in the main toolbar

2 Click the **Spelling and Grammar** icon

3 In the **Spelling and Grammar** dialogue box, review each of the possible errors. You can accept Word's suggested correction by highlighting it and clicking **Change**

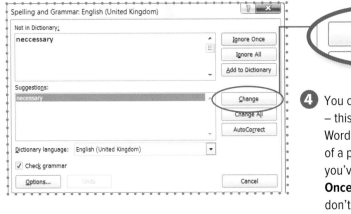

4 You can reject Word's corrections – this is useful, for example, when Word doesn't recognise the spelling of a person's name, or a slang word you've used. Either click **Ignore Once** or **Ignore All** (top right) if you don't want the spellchecker to flag up recurring examples of certain possible errors

ORGANISE YOUR DOCUMENTS

Putting all of your documents in the Documents folder without an ordering system can make finding specific files a little unwieldy. It's worth organising them.

Create sub-folders

1 Press the **Windows key** (see page 13) and **E** to launch Windows Explorer

2 Click on the **Documents** folder

3 Right click in the space below your documents

4 Click **Folder**

5 Click **New**. A new folder will appear in your folder list. Give your new folder a name

RENAME A FILE

1 Right click once on the file you want to rename (you don't need to open it)

2 Click **Rename**

3 Type your new name

4 Press **Enter**

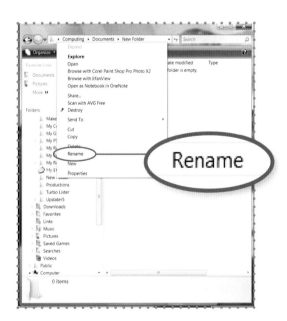

SELECT MULTIPLE FILES OR FOLDERS

You might want to select a number of files at the same time, for example, to be able to delete, copy or print them all.

1 Open the folder that contains the files or folders you want to select

2 Hold down **Ctrl**

3 Click all the items you want to include

4 To change your selection at any point, let go of Ctrl and just click a blank area of the folder window to start again

SEARCH FOR A DOCUMENT

Windows has several default folders for storing files including Documents, Pictures and Music. If you can't find a file, therefore, they're a good place to start your search. If you can't remember where you saved a document, there are a few ways you can search for it.

1 Click 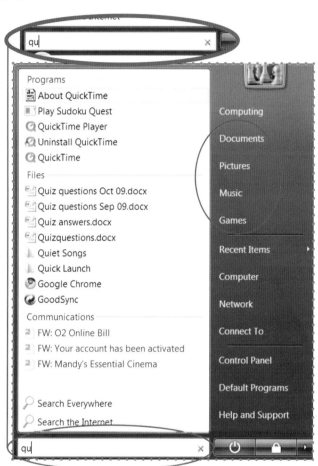 and enter the title of your document in the **Search** box. As you type, files and applications that match what you're typing will appear automatically

2 Alternatively, click on **Pictures**, **Documents** or **Music** in the right-hand pane and a window will open where you can search for particular file types within these folders. In the case of pictures you can also browse the corresponding thumbnails

3 If the search doesn't reveal what you're looking for, click **Advanced Search** – you'll see a clickable link under your search results

4 From here you can search by size, date the file was modified, or even by tags if you're looking for a picture

WORD TIPS

Keyboard shortcuts
There are shortcuts for carrying out common tasks in Word so that you don't have to use your mouse and click on a number of buttons. The following two-button combinations might come in handy.

Ctrl + S to save a document
Ctrl + P to print a document
Ctrl + A to highlight the whole of your document

Or, highlight a specific word/words, then use:
Ctrl + I to italicise text
Ctrl + B to make text bold
Ctrl + U to underline text

Using the format painter
If you've already formatted text and want to apply those same effects to another paragraph:

1 Highlight the text you've already formatted

2 Select the **Home** tab

3 Click on the **Format Painter** icon

4 Select the text you want to apply the formatting to by highlighting it

Use the highlighter pen
Word 2007 contains a high-tech version of a highlighter pen with which you can draw attention to key areas of text.

1 Select your text. Select the **Home** tab and then the highlighter pen ab

2 Click the down arrow to choose the highlighter colour

Undo a mistake

It's easy to get carried away with special effects. But don't panic if you've overdone it. Simply highlight the text in the normal way and click on the **Clear Formatting** icon (it resembles an eraser).

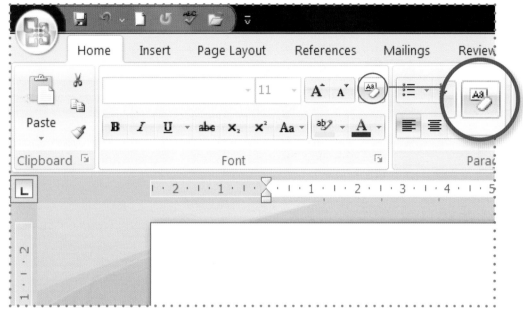

Create wider margins

When you launch a new Microsoft Word document, the Normal template applies the margin widths automatically. However, you can change these if, for instance, you want wider margins.

1 Select the **Page Layout** tab

2 Click on the **Margins** icon

3 Click **Wide** to add bigger margins

Adding columns

Adding columns to a Word document is especially useful if you write a newsletter and want to give your document a magazine feel. To change the number of columns in your document:

1 Click the down arrow beneath the **Columns** icon (within the **Page Layout** tab)

2 Select the number of columns you require from the list that appears

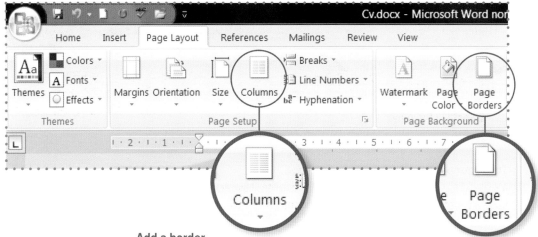

Add a border

Borders are a useful feature to add to your newsletter or party invite.

1 Select the **Page Layout** tab

2 Click on the **Page Borders** icon

3 Select the **Page Border** tab

4 Choose your preferred border style (**Box**, **Shadow**, **3D** or **Custom**). You will see a preview of what your choice will look like in the right-hand side of the window as you click on it

5 Choose your preferred line style under the **Style** heading

6 You can also choose the line colour and width

7 Click **OK** when you've made your selections

Using special effects

You can add a touch of pizzazz to your document with some special effects:

1 Highlight the text you want to change, then right click on it

2 Select **Font**

3 Under the **Effects** section, use the tick boxes to apply effects. You can add a shadow to key words or show them in outline. You can also emboss or engrave them

4 You can also open the Effects menu by clicking on **Effects** in the main toolbar

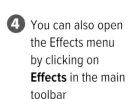
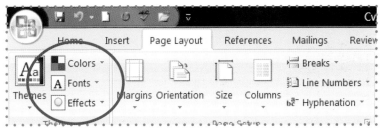

Turn your page from portrait to landscape

It's useful to flip your page on its side (from Portrait to Landscape) if you have a wide table to insert in your document. To do this:

1 Select the **Page Layout** tab

2 Click the drop-down arrow underneath **Orientation**

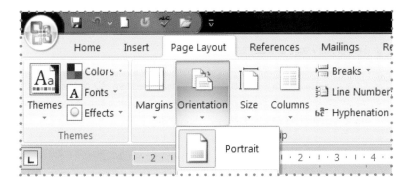

3 Click the **Landscape** icon. You can change it back the same way

Excel

EXCEL EXPLAINED

A spreadsheet application such as Microsoft's Excel 2007 lets you organise information into columns and rows. This is useful for bookkeeping and accounting, and for arranging complicated information into tables and grids.

Tabs – such as Insert, Page Layout, Formulas and Data – provide access to more advanced or specialised options.

The toolbar features the most common Excel functions split into groups such as Font (for basic text editing functions) and Alignment (for controlling text layout), Styles, Number, Cells and Editing.

A cell address is identified by the letter of the column and the number of the row in which it sits. The highlighted cell here is B19, for example.

An Excel file is known as a workbook. It contains a number of spreadsheets (called worksheets). You can swap between different worksheets by clicking on the tabs at the bottom of your screen.

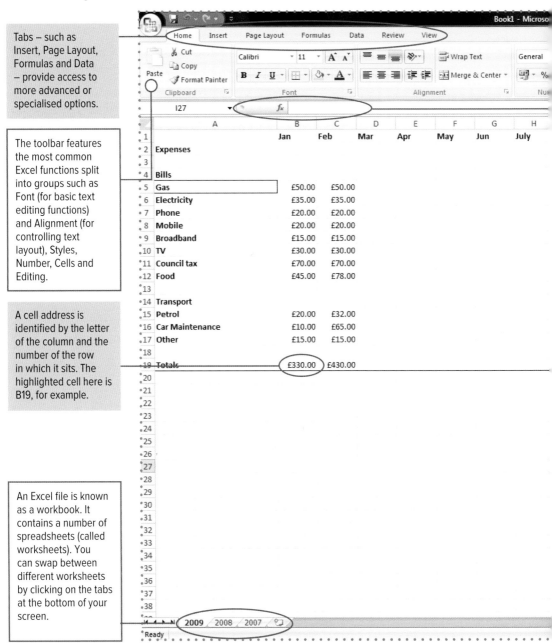

Numerical formulae can be applied in Excel to perform specific mathematical calculations. Excel can also quickly and easily convert information contained in a spreadsheet into a graph or chart.

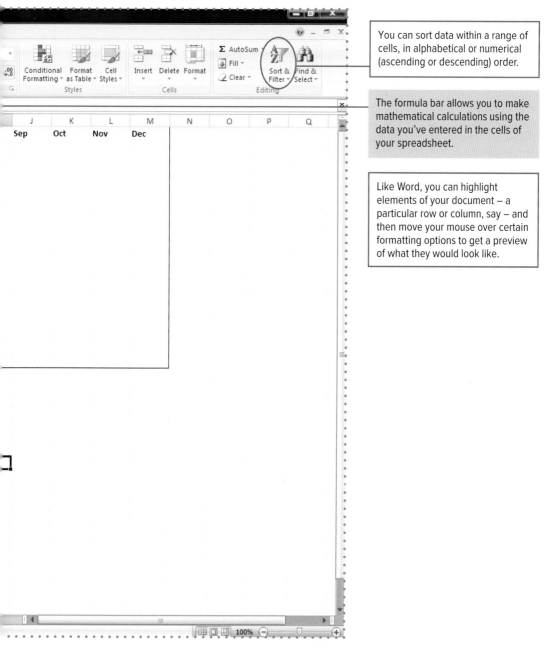

You can sort data within a range of cells, in alphabetical or numerical (ascending or descending) order.

The formula bar allows you to make mathematical calculations using the data you've entered in the cells of your spreadsheet.

Like Word, you can highlight elements of your document – a particular row or column, say – and then move your mouse over certain formatting options to get a preview of what they would look like.

CREATE A BASIC SPREADSHEET

Open a new spreadsheet and enter data

When you open Excel, a blank spreadsheet will automatically open up. You can also open a new blank spreadsheet by following these instructions:

1 Click

2 Click **New**

3 Double click on the **Blank Workbook** icon in the **New Workbook** dialogue box

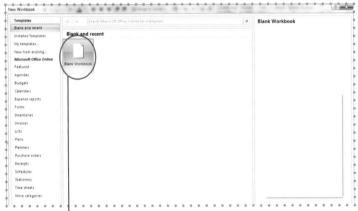

Enter data into a spreadsheet

A spreadsheet is made up of individual blocks known as cells. Cells are identified by row numbers and column letters such as A1 or D14. To enter a piece of data click on a cell and type in your data

You can also enter a heading for your data – click on a cell and type it in

Adjust column width and row height

Your columns may not be wide enough to display all the text you have typed into them, so, to change a single column, move your mouse right to the top of the document so that it's pointing to the line to the right of the column you want to widen.

Your cursor will change to a bold line with arrows pointing left and right. Click and drag the line to the width of the column you want on the left of the line. Then let go. You can do the same for a row – drag the bottom line of the row down to the depth you want in the row above.

You can also set column widths or row heights for your whole
spreadsheet at once:

1 Press **Ctrl + A** on your keyboard to
select all of the spreadsheet

2 Select the **Home** tab

3 Click on the **Format** button in the
Cells section

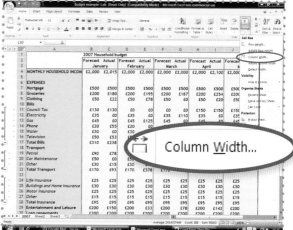

4 Select **Column Width** (or **Row
Height**)

5 A small box will pop up displaying
the current column width (8.43
points by default; row height is 12.75)

6 Enter the value that you require

7 Click **OK**

Add a currency sign

If you're using your spreadsheet to manage your household budget or
other expenses, you'll want to add currency signs to some of your figures.

TRY THIS

You can enter figures for
years, hours etc too. Use
the same steps as adding
a currency sign, but click
on a different format in
the **Category** menu.

1 Select the numbers you want the
change to apply to, then click **Format**
button, as above

2 From the drop-down menu, click
Format Cells

3 Click **Currency** (in the left-hand menu
under the **Number** tab). Use the
up and down arrows to select your
preferred number of decimal places
in the small box on the right

4 Click **OK**

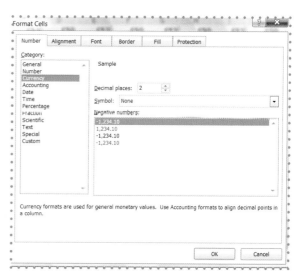

CUSTOMISE YOUR SPREADSHEET

You can customise a document by adding borders, changing background and text colours or choosing new fonts.

Centre text

You may want to centre the text in some of your cells – for example, if they're column headings or titles.

1 Select the cells, columns or rows where you want the text to be centred

2 Right click anywhere in the selected area and select **Format cells**

3 In the box, click the **Alignment** tab

4 Under **Text Alignment**, click the drop-down box under **Horizontal** and select **Center**. This will align the text in your selected cells

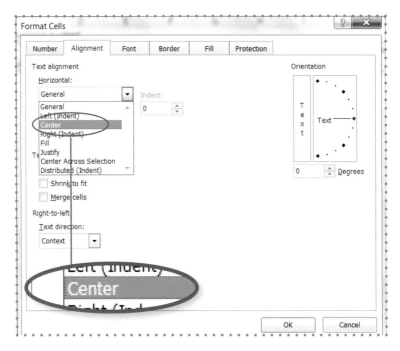

Change font, colour of text or background

1 Follow points 1 and 2 opposite to reach the **Format Cells** box

2 Click the **Font** tab and select the required font from the list. You can also customise the size, style and colour of your text here

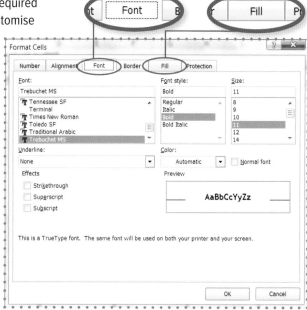

3 To change the cell background colour, ensure the cell or cells you want to change are highlighted, click the **Fill** tab and select a colour of your choice from the palette below **Background Color**. Only the selected area will be shaded in the new colour

4 To choose a different colour for the rest of the cells (single cells, or whole columns/rows), select them separately and do the same. You can also change the colour for the whole spreadsheet by using **Ctrl** + **A** before choosing the colour

5 Click **OK** to see your changes

Add a border

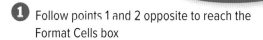

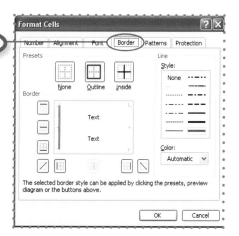

1 Follow points 1 and 2 opposite to reach the Format Cells box

2 Click the **Border** tab

3 Under Presets click both the Outline option and the Inside option

4 Click **OK**

Freeze Panes

When scrolling down a spreadsheet, you can lose sight of the headings at the top of the page, and have to scroll back up to view them. It can be better to keep selected rows or columns in place:

1 Select the row below the one you'd like to freeze

2 Click the **View** tab

3 Click **Freeze Panes** under the Window section

4 Select which option you'd like – for example, 'freeze top row' or 'freeze first column'. Next time you scroll down, the selected area will always appear at the top

Group data

Grouping data allows you to hide certain rows or columns of data (if you only want to see a summary of all the bills you pay, for example, rather than each individual one).

1 Select the row or column you want to collapse

2 Select the **Data** tab on the top toolbar

NEXT STEP

Want your spreadsheet to do some calculations for you? Find out how to use formulae on page 64.

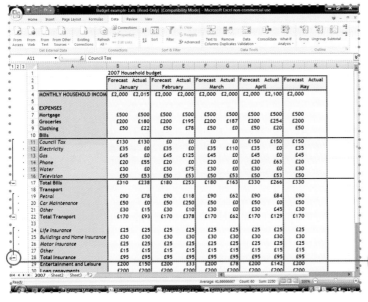

3 Click **Group**, then click **Group** again on the drop-down menu

4 Click the minus sign beneath the black outline bar to hide the data

5 Click on the plus sign when you want to show it again

ADD UP A COLUMN OF FIGURES

You can use a formula to make calculations based on what you've entered into your spreadsheet. Here's how to add up a column or row of figures:

1 Highlight the row or column of figures you want to add up by clicking on the first one, holding down the mouse button and dragging it, letting go when you reach the last one, so that you've highlighted all the cells you want

TRY THIS

If you select a vertical list rather than specific numbers then click **AutoSum**, Excel will highlight the numbers it thinks you want to add together. If it's correct, click **AutoSum** again or press **Enter** to complete the calculation.

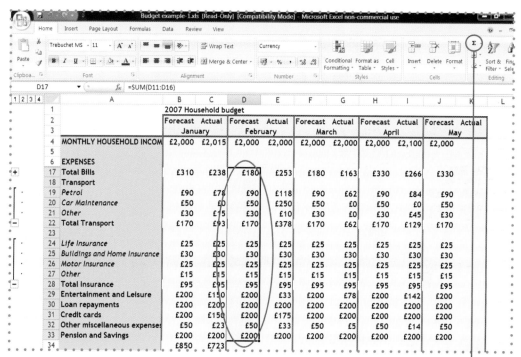

2 Click on the **AutoSum** button (under **Editing** in the **Home** tab toolbar)

3 The total sum of all the values in your selection will be displayed in the cell directly underneath the value for your final, highlighted cell, in this case February's forecast (in cell D34)

WRITE A SIMPLE FORMULA

Excel's mathematical skills aren't confined to addition. So, if, for example, you want to find out how much money you've got left to spend after subtracting your outgoings from your income, Excel can help by using a formula.

A formula always starts with an = sign, and uses cell references to identify data to be included in the calculation. A typical formula might be =(D6-F4)*G8 (the asterisk represents multiplication). If D6 is 10, F4 is 6 and G8 is 2, the result will be 8.

At first glance, these formulae can seem complicated, but stick with it. Excel formulae follow the standard order of mathematical operations we all learnt at school – hence the brackets to indicate the part of the calculation that needs to be performed first. The formula bar shows the address of the selected cell on the left-hand side.

TIP
Add a row or column of figures by simply clicking on the **Autosum** icon. See page 63 for more details.

To calculate

1 Click on the cell where you want the answer to your calculation to appear

2 Enter your formula in the formula bar – for example, =C4-C34

3 The answer will appear in the cell you selected. When you make changes to other cells that appear in the formula – in this case, if you change either C4 or C34 – Excel will automatically recalculate the new figure

USING THE INTERNET

By reading and following all the steps in this chapter, you will get to grips with:

- **Setting up a broadband connection**

- **Surfing the internet**

- **Buying items online**

YOUR INTERNET OPTIONS

To get online you'll need an internet connection. This used to mean having a dial-up connection that used an existing phone line – it was slow and you couldn't use your phone at the same time. Most people can now connect using broadband – it provides a much faster service and allows you to phone and be online at the same time. There are three types of broadband.

ADSL Broadband

ADSL (asymmetric digital subscriber line) broadband uses BT's copper wire phone network and is available to more than 99 per cent of UK households. To get ADSL broadband, you must have a fixed BT phone line.

However, BT is not the only choice of phone provider – line-rental providers such as the Post Office, TalkTalk and Tiscali also use BT's network and offer their own broadband packages. Some providers also offer discounts for getting your phone and broadband together. Typically, advertised download speeds range from 0.5 to up to 20 megabits per second (Mbps). But the speed you'll actually get depends on many factors – for example, the distance you are from the phone exchange and the amount of traffic (other people using broadband via that exchange).

Pros
- ▶ Big choice of providers and packages
- ▶ Local loop unbundling (see below) means potential speeds are increasing and prices are dropping

Cons
- ▶ Some limitations on speed
- ▶ You must pay a fixed-phone line rental

Who is it for?
Anyone with a fixed BT line who wants choice in providers and packages.

Local loop unbundling
Local loop unbundling (LLU) is a type of ADSL broadband where internet service providers (ISPs) install their own equipment in BT exchanges. The ISPs still use BT wires but adding their own equipment enables them to offer faster/cheaper broadband. Availability is limited to, at most, 70 per cent of UK households, often in more populated areas.

TRY THIS

If you have a BT line, you can get a provisional guide on what broadband speeds your phone line should be able to support – enter your phone number on www. dslchecker.bt.com/adsl

Cable broadband

Cable broadband, which is currently offered only by Virgin Media, provides an equivalent service to ADSL. It's available to around 50 per cent of UK homes, mostly in urban areas. It offers a range of maximum broadband speeds from 2 to 50Mbps. You don't need a BT line, but may need to have a Virgin phone line installed.

Virgin claims that distance from the exchange doesn't affect its broadband speeds, but this doesn't necessarily mean you'll get advertised speeds, which are still affected by equipment or traffic at peak times.

Virgin offers some very cheap 'bundling' deals to cable customers taking two or more services (broadband, home phone, digital TV and mobile).

Pros
▶ Speed isn't affected by distance from exchanges
▶ Cable fibre quality means the potential speed is higher than ADSL
▶ A trial has found that up to 50Mbps is possible
▶ Broadband bundles are competitively priced
▶ If you don't have a fixed line a Virgin one is cheaper to install than a BT one

Cons
▶ Only available to half of UK households
▶ Only one choice of provider
▶ Cable broadband has many of the same speed limitations as ADSL

Who is it for?
Price-conscious consumers, particularly those who want a bundle with digital TV, phone and/or mobile. Also those who live a fair distance from a BT exchange but want to achieve reasonable broadband speeds.

Mobile broadband
Mobile broadband allows anyone with a Mac or Windows laptop to get online wherever they are. The key to getting online is a USB modem (dongle) that plugs into your computer's USB port and lets your computer connect to the internet using a data connection such as 3G. Mobile broadband is growing in popularity.

Dongle
A small device that connects to a computer's USB port. In this context, it enables you to connect to the internet.

NEXT STEP

If you have broadband and you're not happy with your service, find out how to switch at page 79.

▶ Getting Connected

GET BROADBAND

If you don't have an internet connection already, you can get ADSL broadband by taking these steps:

1 Check that ADSL broadband is available in your area. If you have a friend with an internet connection, you can check on www.broadbandchecker.co.uk by typing in your postcode. Alternatively, phone a broadband provider you'd like to use and check with them

2 Once you've chosen a broadband provider, phone them to discuss which package best suits your needs

3 Find out from them what speed you can expect to get at your address and if there are any other conditions – such as a cap on how much you can download. Also check their pricing structure

4 In most cases your ISP will provide a router or modem as part of the deal. Check that this is the case

5 Once you've agreed to the conditions of your ISP contract, your line will be upgraded so that it can carry the data signal for ADSL broadband and voice calls at the same time. This is known as line activation and is usually done remotely. There may be a charge and you'll usually have to wait about a week for the ISP to do this

6 Once your line has been activated and you've received your router or modem, you'll need to connect it and configure your computer. Some ISPs offer a service where they send an engineer to do this. For others, you follow instructions on a CD. See page 70 for tips on setting up your computer

Jargon buster

ISP
An internet service provider (ISP) is the company that enables and services your connection to the internet.

Getting broadband if you already have dial-up internet

1 Choose a broadband provider as above, and find out from them how long it will take for broadband activation

2 Cancel your dial-up internet subscription (subject to your contract terms and notice period), timing it so you won't be left without internet access for long. If you use a pay-as-you-go dial-up internet service, you don't need to cancel

3 Ask your chosen broadband provider to activate your broadband, then install your modem and configure your computer as normal. See page 70 for more details on this

See page 70 for more details on this

Jargon buster ▶

Modem
A device that allows a computer to send information over a telephone line.

getting connected

▶ Getting Connected

CONNECT YOUR EQUIPMENT

Set up your router

Many providers will send you a booklet/CD to help you set up your connection. For a router with in-built modem, it's likely to include these steps:

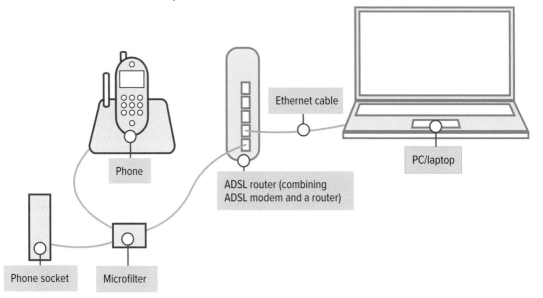

Ethernet cable

PC/laptop

Phone

ADSL router (combining ADSL modem and a router)

Phone socket   Microfilter

Jargon buster ▶

Microfilter
A device that attaches to your telephone socket and enables you to make voice calls and use broadband at the same time, via ADSL.

1 Attach a microfilter to the main phone socket (where the phone line enters the house)

2 You should have all the cables you need included in the box with the router. Plug one end of the modem cable into the relevant microfilter socket. Plug the other end into the back of your router

3 Your telephone also plugs into the microfilter. This means that you can be on the phone while also having an active broadband connection

4 Now connect your router's power supply and switch it on

Connect your router to the computer

1 The easiest way to connect your router to your PC or laptop is via an ethernet cable (this will come in the router box)

2 Put one end of the ethernet cable into the socket on the PC and the other end into one of the four identical sockets on the router

Accessing your router's setup

To configure your router, follow these steps:

1 Start up your computer and open your web browser to access your router settings

2 Enter the address of your router into the browser's address bar. This is a number listed in your manual. In the case of many routers, this number is 192.168.1.1

3 Press **Enter**

4 You will then be asked for login details. Your default username and password will be in your manual

Jargon buster

Router
A device that routes data between computers and other devices. Routers can connect computers to each other or connect them to the internet.

Change your settings

1 You'll see a page that looks like a web page – this is the router set-up page. From here you can make changes to the router

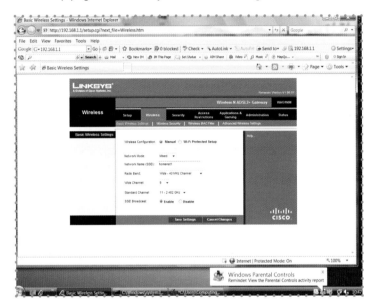

2 To change the default password, click the **Administration** tab, enter a password in the password window, confirm it and save

3 For the router to connect to the internet you need to configure the ADSL part of it with the right settings. Click on the **Setup** tab

4 The router will ask for your ISP user name and password. Enter these – again, they should have been provided by your ISP

5 You may be asked to enter details about 'encapsulation' or 'multiplexing'. You don't need to know what these mean. Simply ask your internet service provider about what you should see in these settings

6 Scroll down and save your changes

7 You should now be able to connect to the internet on the PC connected to the router. If you don't want to connect any PCs wirelessly, then you're done

SET UP WIRELESS BROADBAND

Once you've set up your broadband connection with cables (see page 70), you have the option to go wireless if your router supports it. This means that your computer will not need to be physically connected in order to use the broadband connection. A wireless network uses a type of radio wave to transmit data between machines without the need for cables. Each computer is connected to a central router by ethernet cables.

Set up a wireless network

To set up a wireless (Wi-Fi) network you'll need a central wireless router plus a wireless adaptor for each of the PCs or devices you want to connect. Some computers (particularly laptops) may already be wireless enabled. Check your computer's specifications (see page 208) to see if this is the case. If not, the easiest method is to plug in a USB adaptor. You can buy one of these small devices from a computer shop.

1 In the router set-up page, click the **Wireless** tab

2 In the **Network Name (SSID)** field change the name of your network to something memorable like 'Home wireless'

(see page 70)

USB
A way of connecting that allows you to transfer data easily. Many devices are connected to a computer via USB cables.

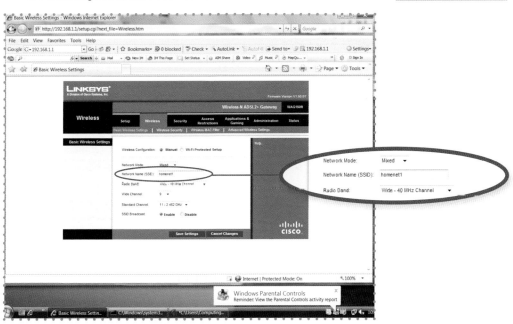

getting connected

3 Choose the **Wireless Security** option. From here you can turn on security for your new wireless network

4 Select **WPA** or **WPA-Personal** from the drop-down menu (the options will differ depending on your router) and enter a pass phrase (this works the same as a password)

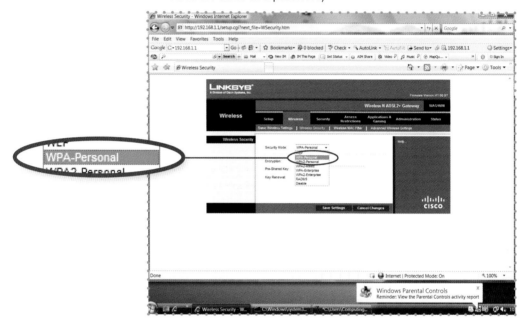

5 Save your settings and unplug the ethernet cable

6 The computer you're trying to connect wirelessly should automatically detect wireless networks within its range. A message will pop up in the taskbar to notify you. Click on it and you will see a list of available wireless networks. Yours will show up under the name you gave it earlier

TIP
For more on securing your wireless network, see page 77.

7 Select your wireless network from the list (usually by double-clicking on it) and connect to it

8 You'll be prompted to enter your security pass phrase. Once you've done this, you'll be connected to your wireless network and can surf the internet

CONNECT TO OTHER COMPUTERS

When multiple computers are connected together, it's often referred to as a home network. You can share all kinds of data over a network – from documents and emails to music, photos and video. If you have a broadband internet connection, a network means that all the computers in your household can access the web at the same time.

Once you've set up your wireless broadband connection on one computer (see page 73), you're ready to connect other computers.

Install your wireless adaptors

1 Each PC will need its own wireless adaptor and the set-up procedure will differ depending on the make, model and type of adaptor

2 During the set-up procedure, follow onscreen instructions, making sure that you put a tick next to **Infrastructure Mode** and that you enter the name (SSID) of your wireless network

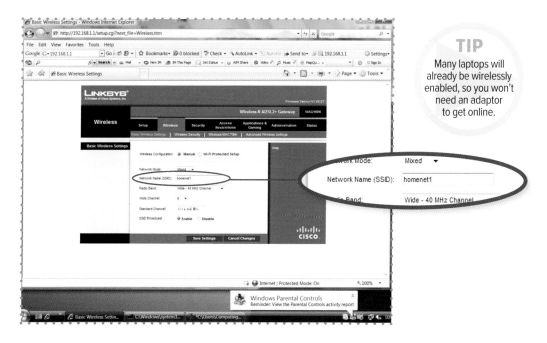

TIP
Many laptops will already be wirelessly enabled, so you won't need an adaptor to get online.

3 If you have secured your wireless network, you will need to enter your encryption authorisation key when you are connecting to the network

4 You can test your connection at this stage by opening your browser and trying to view a web page

Set up your workgroup
You'll now need to set up a Windows Workgroup, so your PCs can talk to each other. Firstly, turn on all of the computers and devices (for example, printers) that you want to be part of your network

1 On one of your computers, click

2 Click **Control Panel**

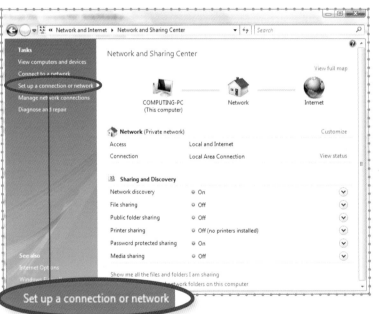

3 Click **Network and Internet**

4 Click **Network and Sharing Center**

5 In the left pane, click **Set up a connection or network**

6 Follow the steps that appear onscreen that will guide you through the process of adding other computers

NEXT STEP ▶

Now you've set up a broadband connection, you can get online. See page 84 for advice on surfing the internet.

7 Carry out the same steps on each of the other computers

SECURE YOUR WIRELESS NETWORK

Wireless networks are far more convenient than traditional, wired ones, but they bring with them certain security risks. It's important that you take precautions to stop people connecting to your network, or even changing your network settings, without your knowledge. Keep your network secure by taking these steps:

▶ All wireless networks have a name (sometimes called the SSID – see page 73) that you can change when you set up your router. Make it something that doesn't give any clues to your identity, or to the type of router that you're using

▶ If your router doesn't broadcast the network name (or SSID), it is more difficult for anyone looking for a network to connect to it. If you won't often be connecting new devices to your network, consider turning off the router's broadcast SSID option

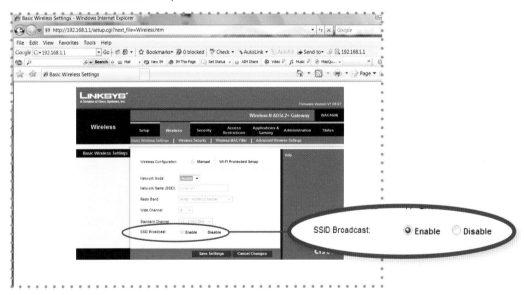

▶ Many routers come with weak passwords like 'admin', which are easy for other people to guess. Change it to something more difficult

▶ You can encrypt your network to make it more secure. Your router instruction manual should show you how. Bear in mind that the older system (WEP) isn't as secure as the newest system (WPA) but even that is much better than nothing

▶ If all the computers you need to connect are near the router, then why not connect via cables? Turn off the wireless network from the router and nobody else will be able to connect wirelessly

TIPS ON USING YOUR ROUTER

Get to grips with your router by taking note of these tips.

▶ Get the router working with a wired connection (using an ethernet cable), before setting up wirelessly

▶ Remember you can reset the router to its original settings if you make a mistake or forget the set-up password. You can usually do this by holding down the reset button for a count of 10 seconds

▶ Connect the router to the phone socket that's nearest to where the line enters your house. Any additional distance can reduce signal quality and may affect your broadband connection

▶ Don't forget to install microfilters in your telephone sockets. Every device in your house that's connected to a phone socket (including phones and faxes) will need one

▶ Give your network a name that won't reveal your identity, location or the make of your router

▶ Your router will be able to tell you all sorts of information about what it's doing. Clicking on the **Status** tab on the router's home page will let you see, for instance, whether your ADSL connection is active, and at what speed, or which computers are connected

SWITCH BROADBAND PROVIDER

Before starting any switching process, you should talk to your current provider. If you switch broadband provider before the end of any minimum contract term, you may have to pay a hefty broadband cancellation fee. As long as you're outside your minimum contract period, however, your broadband provider will be keen to keep your custom and may well offer you a much more attractive deal.

The process you use to switch internet suppliers will vary depending on whether you're just switching broadband, or whether you're changing your home phone service at the same time as your broadband.

Switch between ADSL broadband providers

If you are switching to and from ADSL broadband (broadband via a BT phone line), you'll need to use the MAC (migration authorisation code) process. A MAC is a unique code that identifies a particular broadband line.

1 Ask your existing broadband provider for your broadband MAC. Make sure you stress you are only asking for your MAC and not cancelling your broadband account; some broadband providers will see requesting your MAC as a sign you want to cancel the service, which is bad if you change your mind

2 Your broadband provider must provide a MAC on request and should send you the MAC within five working days. Your broadband MAC is valid for 30 days from the date it's issued

3 Give your MAC to the broadband internet provider you want to switch to. They should process your request and give you a transfer date

4 If you have problems switching between broadband providers because of difficulties obtaining a MAC from your existing broadband supplier, take a look at Ofcom's advice (www.ofcom.org.uk/complain/internet/switching/)

getting connected

Switch to or from cable broadband

Cable broadband provider Virgin Media does not use the MAC broadband switching process. If you're switching your broadband service to or from Virgin Media, you simply cancel your existing broadband service and sign up to your new broadband service. You may need to have a new broadband line installed.

Switch your phone and broadband services simultaneously

If you're switching to or from a provider that offers phone and broadband services bundled together, you may not be able to use the MAC broadband switching process for technical reasons.

However, under Ofcom's switching regulations, phone and broadband bundle providers are still required to make the switch as easy for you as possible. You can find detailed advice on the various broadband and phone switching processes on Ofcom's website (www.ofcom.org.uk).

Each of the three processes aims for the minimum possible disruption, though there is a chance you may experience some loss of service. In each case, ask your new supplier which broadband and phone switching process to use and how long the switch will take.

CONNECT DEVICES

When you connect a new printer, scanner, webcam or other device to your computer, you need to install the software that comes with it (the driver).

1 Plug the external device into the mains power supply with the cable provided

2 A new device often comes with its own driver on CD. Insert the CD into your computer's disc drive

3 An installation wizard will start up – this will guide you through the process of installing the software. Follow the instructions on screen

If you experience problems with a device, you can reinstall the driver using the Device Manager.

1 Click then **Control Panel**

2 Click **System and Maintenance**

3 Scroll down and click **Device Manager**

4 Double click on the heading under which your device would fall, then right click on the device driver you want to remove

5 Click **Uninstall**

6 In the **Confirm Device Uninstall** window click **OK**

7 If asked whether you want to restart, click **Yes,** or manually restart the computer. This will reinstall the device driver automatically

TRY THIS

Over time, drivers are updated – new features may be added and any problems that are found will be fixed. If you're having trouble getting a device to work, check the manufacturer's website for an updated driver.

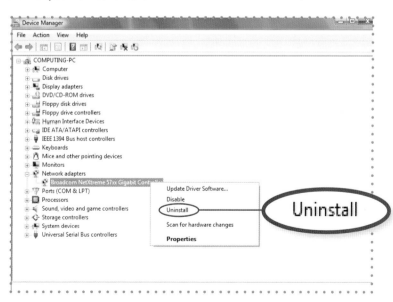

⏵ Surfing the internet

YOUR WEB BROWSER

Your browser is your window on the web. It allows you to view and navigate between web pages. But there's a lot more your web browser can do too, such as storing your favourite web pages and protecting you from common internet scams.

There are four main web browsers available:
- ▶ Microsoft's Internet Explorer (IE)
- ▶ Mozilla Firefox
- ▶ Opera Browser
- ▶ Safari

Internet Explorer comes free with versions of Microsoft Vista and, as such, is a popular consumer choice.

Main Internet Explorer
Includes File, Edit, View etc. Press the **Alt** key if the menu bar goes missing.

Address Bar
This is where you type the address of the web page you want to visit.

Favorites
Here you can bookmark the websites you visit regularly (see page 92).

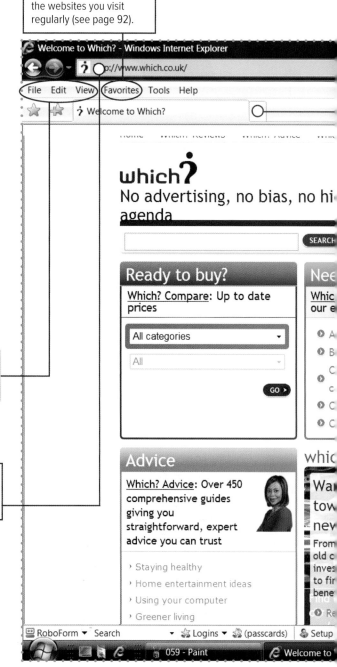

Multiple tabs
Tabs let you view different web pages without closing the first one. Click here to launch a new tab or press **Ctrl + T.** For more on tabbed browsing see page 85.

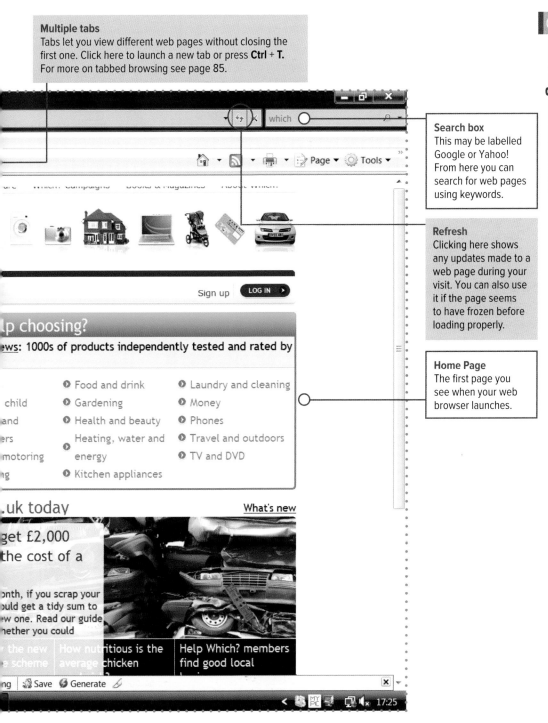

Search box
This may be labelled Google or Yahoo! From here you can search for web pages using keywords.

Refresh
Clicking here shows any updates made to a web page during your visit. You can also use it if the page seems to have frozen before loading properly.

Home Page
The first page you see when your web browser launches.

▶ Surfing the internet

ENTER A WEB ADDRESS

Every web page has its own web address, often referred to as the URL (Uniform Resource Locator). For example, the Which? website is http://www.which.co.uk. If you already know the web address for a page, follow the steps below; if you need to search for one, see page 92.

1 Type the full address into the address bar

2 Press **Enter**

NAVIGATE WEB PAGES

Back and forward buttons

As you move between web pages, Internet Explorer keeps track of the pages you've viewed. You can return to the last page you looked at by clicking the **Back** button. Click it several times to go back a number of pages. Once you've clicked the **Back** button, you can also use the **Forward** button to return.

Recent pages

Rather than repeatedly clicking the Back and Forward buttons, you can use the **Recent Pages** menu to revisit a page you've looked at recently. Click the arrow next to the Forward button and select a website from the list.

Links

Most web pages contain links to other pages. Click on a link and the relevant web page will open up. Links will often appear in a different colour, or as underlined text. To check whether something is a link, hover your cursor over it – if the mouse pointer turns into a pointing finger it's a link and you can click on it.

Tabbed browsing

Tabbed browsing allows you to open multiple web pages at the same time within the same browser window. This can aid navigation by letting you open a link in a fresh tab (right click the link and select **Open in new tab**), while keeping the old page open as a reference.

You can switch between tabs by clicking on the one you want along the top edge of the main window. To close a tab, click on it to highlight it and then click the grey 'X'.

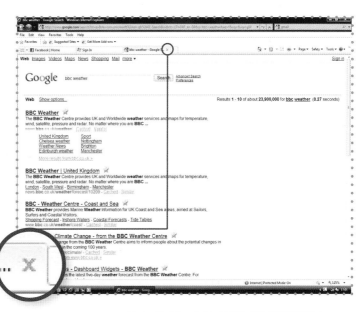

SEARCH THE WEB

If you want to look at a website but don't know the exact website address, you can search the internet using a search engine. Using a search engine is also useful if you just want to find information on a specific topic rather than find a specific site.

The most popular search engine is Google (www.google.co.uk), but there are other options such as Yahoo (www.yahoo.com) or Microsoft's search engine (www.bing.com). You can type one of these addresses into the address bar to take you to the home page and enter your search from there.

Alternatively, if you're using the latest versions of web browsers Internet Explorer or Firefox, you will already have an instant search box located to the side of the address bar on your web browser.

1 Click once in the **Search** box in the top, right-hand corner of the toolbar

2 Type what you're looking for and press **Enter**

3 Results will be displayed on screen

4 If you can't see what you're looking for, click **Next** at the bottom of the page to see more results. Or change the search terms to widen or tighten the search

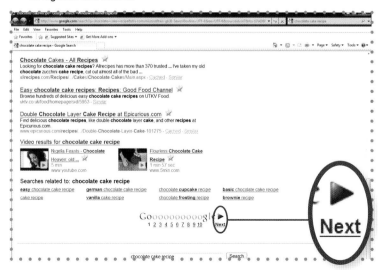

Add another search engine box

If you don't want to use the default search engine that appears on your web browser, you can switch to a different search engine, or add a specialist search engine box, for example, an eBay box, which will just search within the eBay site.

1 Click the arrow to the right of the magnifying glass icon and click **Find More Providers**

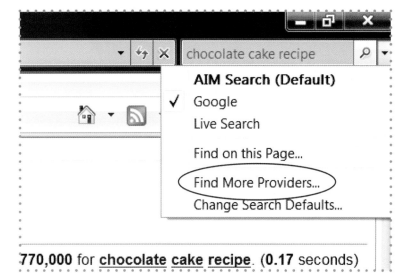

2 You'll see a list of options. Choose the one you want and click **Add to Internet Explorer**

3 Or click **Create your own Search Provider** to add one of your own that isn't in the list of options

4 When you next want to switch to a different search engine box, click the arrow next to the magnifying glass to show the list

5 Click on the search engine you want to use. Then in the box enter the word/s you want to search for and press **Enter**

► Surfing the internet

► Using standard punctuation in your searches will make them more efficient. For instance, putting double quotes around a key phrase – "John Smith", for example – restricts results to only those where the words appear together. Without the quotes a search would return results such as 'St John's, Smith Square'

► If you aren't sure whether a word has a hyphen in it or not (email or e-mail), keep the hyphen in; most search engines will check all variations

► Adding a + or - symbol will keep or remove certain words or phrases from search results. So, if you want to search for an Egyptian-themed hotel in Las Vegas, type Egypt + "Las Vegas"

► Searches won't include the/a etc so you don't need to include these

► You can restrict searches to certain websites. For example, you can look up a computer error code on Microsoft's website by putting the code you're searching for in the search box and following it with site:microsoft.com. The search engine will search results from Microsoft's website only

► If the web address you're typing ends in .com, you only need to type the words between the www. and .com and press **Ctrl + ENTER**. For example, type BBC in the address bar and then press **Ctrl + ENTER**

► You don't have to type http:// every time you want to visit a website. If you type everything after the last forward slash, Internet Explorer will fill in the rest. For example, just type www.bbc.com rather than http://www.bbc.com

Search for images and files

Search engines automatically search for text results first so, if you want to search for images, follow the relevant link or button (usually labelled 'Images') on your search engine's home page. Type in the key words relating to the image you're looking for and press **Enter**.

You can also specify the types of documents you want to search for. For example you can narrow your search, so that your results only include PowerPoint presentations or PDF files – both popular file types. Follow the **Options** or **Advanced settings** links from your search engine's home page.

In Google, a quick way to search by file type is to include the word filetype: followed by the three-letter file extension of your desired file, followed by the key words. Here are some examples of what to type:

filetype:pdf – Searches PDF files
filetype:doc – Searches Word documents
filetype:ppt – Searches PowerPoint files

Remember to include key words in the search query too (such as filetype: pdf BBC Annual Report).

Jargon buster

File extension
The letters that appear after a file name. They show what type of document it is.

⏵ Surfing the internet

CHANGE YOUR HOME PAGE

Your home page is the first web page you see whenever you open the internet. This is usually set to a default page, but can easily be changed, for example, if you like a particular news site, always use webmail (see page 114) or keep up to date with a blog.

① Go to the web page you'd like to use as your home page

② Click the arrow to the right of the **Home button**, and then click **Add or Change Home Page**

③ Click **Yes** to save your changes

④ To go to the home page at any time, click the **House** icon

If you change your mind, you can reset the home page back to the default. In Internet Explorer, for example:

① Click **Tools**, and then click **Internet Options**

② Click the **General** tab

③ Click **Use default** to replace your current home page with the one that was used when you first installed Internet Explorer

④ Click **Apply** to save your changes

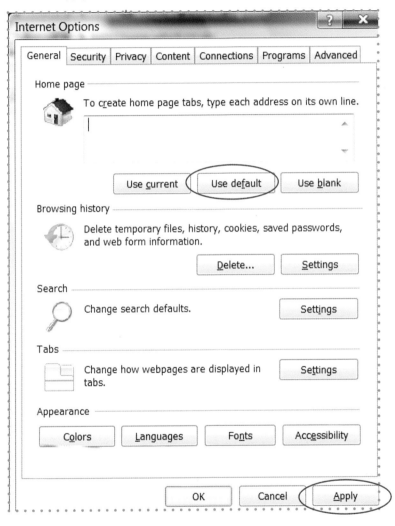

⑤ Click **OK**

BOOKMARK SITES

Web browsers allow you to bookmark your favourite websites. In Internet Explorer they will be stored under Favorites and you will be able to click on them to open the website quickly without having to type the address into the address bar.

To bookmark a new website:

1 Go to the website you want to add

2 Click the **Favorites** button

3 Click **Add to favorites** in the drop-down menu

4 In the box that appears, type a name for the website and click **Add**

TIP
To rename a link or folder, right click on it, then click **Rename**. Type the new name and press **Enter**.

Add a Favorite ✕

⭐ **Add a Favorite**
Add this webpage as a favorite. To access your favorites, visit the Favorites Center.

Name: Which? website

Create in: ⭐ Favorites ▼ New Folder

Add Cancel

To open one of your favourite web pages in Internet Explorer:

TIP
To move a link or folder, click on it and drag it to the new position or folder.

1 Click the **Favorites** button ⭐

2 Click the **Favorites** tab if it's not already selected

3 In the **Favorites** list, click the web page that you want to open

MANAGE YOUR BOOKMARKED SITES

You can organise your favourite websites into separate folders, making them easier to find than if they are in one long list.

1 In Internet Explorer, click the **Favorites** button

2 Click **Organize favorites**

3 In the dialogue box that appears you'll see a list of your favourite links and folders

4 Click on a folder to expand it and see the links it contains

5 To create a new folder, click **New Folder** When a folder icon appears, right click on it.

6 Click **Rename** and type a name for it (for example, Holiday websites) and press **Enter**

7 When you've finished, click **Close**

TIP
To delete a link or folder, right click on it, click **Delete**, then click **Yes**.

surfing the internet

INTERNET EXPLORER TIPS

▶ Flick back and forwards between web pages you've visited by pressing the **Shift key** and using the scroll wheel on the top of your mouse (up is forwards, down is backwards on the scroll wheel)

▶ Change the size of the text on a web page by clicking **Page** (to the right of the tabs) on the toolbar and then **Zoom**. You can then select from various percentage sizes

▶ To search for a specific word or phrase on a web page you're visiting, press **Ctrl + F** and enter the word or phrase

Access parental controls
Internet Explorer includes controls to help protect your children online.

1 Go to **Tools** in the main internet toolbar

2 Click **Internet Options**

3 Click on the **Content** tab and then click **Parental controls**. You can then choose which to apply

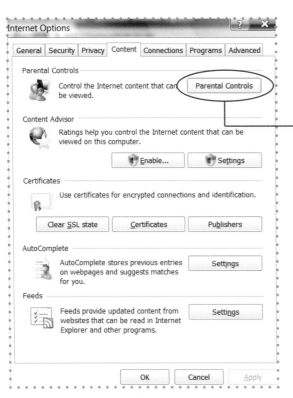

Delete browsing history
Internet Explorer stores a history of all the websites you have visited. You can delete this information to save space on your computer or to protect your privacy

1 With your Internet Explorer window open, click **Tools**

2 Click **Internet Options**

3 Click **Delete Browsing History**

4 Under **History,** click **Delete History**, then click **Yes** to confirm that you want to delete the history

5 Click **Close**

General internet shortcuts

These may be useful to save having to click on a number of buttons.

F11	Turns Full Screen Mode on or off (removing the toolbar and taskbar, or reinstating them)
TAB	Moves the cursor through the Address Bar, Refresh button, Search Box etc until you reach the item you want
Ctrl + F	Finds a word or phrase on a web page
Ctrl + N	Opens the current web page in a new window
Ctrl + P	Prints the page
Ctrl + A	Selects all items on the page
Ctrl + PLUS SIGN	Zooms in
Ctrl + MINUS SIGN	Zooms out
Ctrl + 0	Zooms to 100 per cent

Internet navigation shortcuts

Alt + HOME	Goes to the home page
Alt + LEFT	Goes back a page
Alt + RIGHT	Goes forward a page
F5	Refreshes a page (see page 83)
ESC	Stops downloading a page

Tab shortcuts

Ctrl + Q	Opens Quick Tab view (so you can see all of the tabs you have open)
Ctrl + T	Opens a new tab
Ctrl + SHIFT + Q	Shows list of open tabs
Ctrl + TAB	Switches to next tab
Ctrl + SHIFT + TAB	Switches to previous tab

▶ Online Activities

ONLINE ACTIVITIES

Once you're online, there are a number of very useful things you can do, such as shopping, banking and sharing information.

CREATE AN EBAY ACCOUNT

eBay is a website that allows you to buy and sell items – the online equivalent of the newspaper's classified pages. Before you can start advertising or buying, you'll need an account.

1 Go to the eBay home page at www.ebay.co.uk

2 Click on **Register**

3 Enter your name, address and email address

4 Choose a username

BID ON EBAY

An eBay auction works like a normal auction – the highest bidder wins
– but in this case it takes place over a few days and has a cut-off time.

1 Find the item that you want to bid on and click on it

2 Enter the amount you want to bid and click on **Place Bid**

3 Ensure that your bid is higher than the current one then click **Confirm Bid** (by doing so, you agree to buy the item if you are successful)

Alternatively, you can enter the maximum that you are prepared to pay
for the item and eBay's proxy bidding service will automatically bid
incrementally on your behalf up to that amount. If your bid is the highest
at the cut-off time then you've won the auction.

If your bid is successful you'll be told by email. It will contain details of the
types of payment that the seller accepts: credit or debit card or PayPal, for
example. To use PayPal, you'll need to sign up for a PayPal account. For
more on this see page 101.

BE CAREFUL

Some sellers may ask you
to pay via money transfer
service Western Union.
Don't. eBay has banned
the use of these
transactions on the
website because money
transfers leave no
electronic paper trail or
proof of payment.

SELL ON EBAY

To sell an item on eBay, you'll need to log on to the website and press the **Sell** button. Then you need to follow the on-screen instructions to fill in the details of your item. The better you do this, the more money someone is likely to bid.

Here are a few simple tips you can use to make your auction stand out from the crowd.

TRY THIS

eBay has a community of users who discuss their top selling tips on the online forums. Check out your favourite sales categories at http://groups.ebay.co.uk or ask other members for advice at http://pages.ebay.co.uk/community/answercenter.

▶ One of the first decisions you'll need to make is in which category to list your item. If you're unsure, type in a few key words about it and eBay will suggest a category for you. It's possible to list products in multiple categories to give them more exposure – but your listing fees will be doubled as a result (for more on these fees see Costs, opposite)

▶ Each eBay listing has a one-line title and you'll need to choose a catchy title to grab people's attention. Buyers will typically conduct title searches, and results will be listed according to relevance. The more information you provide, the more chance there is that potential buyers will click through to your item

▶ It's essential that you include a photograph of your item. Buyers want to be able to see what they're buying and it gives them a good indication of its condition. The first photograph is free, additional ones will cost more. Make sure your pictures are clear and well-lit

▶ Keep descriptions (including the title) upfront and honest, while remaining positive and upbeat about the item

▶ Remember to get the brand/model names and spelling variations correct

▶ Don't forget to list all postage information and returns policies clearly. For example, if you're willing to post your item overseas you can quote a separate postage cost for this

▶ Make sure your listing ends when traffic to eBay is busiest as it'll attract last-minute bids. Weekends and weekday evenings usually attract the most buyers

► Research how much items have sold for in the past by browsing 'completed items' and learn from other sellers' successful listings

► Start your bidding at a low price – it will attract more people to place a bid (you can choose what price to start your item at when you first list it)

► Always respond to bidders' enquiries in a timely manner

► Build up a reputation selling smaller value items. The higher your feedback rating, the more people are likely to trust you (see page 100 for more on feedback ratings)

Costs

You'll have to pay to list your item on eBay just as you'd pay for a classified advertisement in a newspaper. eBay charges two types of fee: listing fees (the cost to insert your item; this depends on its starting price) and final value fees (a commission based on the price your item sells for). See http://pages.ebay.co.uk/help/sell/fees.html for details of all the latest prices.

Postage and packaging

Post and packaging prices are paid for by the buyer but as a seller you need to list these charges upfront. To work out what these will be, you will need to weigh your item along with all your packaging and make sure you've measured the package's exact dimensions. Then consult the Royal Mail website (www.royalmail.com) to determine your shipping charges – these will differ depending on the level of postage you are offering (1st or 2nd class or Special Delivery, say).

It's more environmentally conscious to recycle packaging, so you can make your sales more attractive by passing on these cost savings, or even offering postage and packaging for free as an incentive for buyers to bid on your item.

You can also offer post and packaging prices for those bidding in other countries (this is optional). If you want to do this, remember to add alternative postal charges in the relevant section when listing your item.

BE CAREFUL

eBay allows buyers to leave you feedback, which is added to your feedback rating. It's important to ensure that you have a good rating as buyers often check before choosing to bid. Selling a few, smaller value items is a quick way to increase your score.

eBay feedback ratings

Buyers are asked to leave feedback on the transaction. This includes a short comment and a positive, neutral or negative rating. During the auction, you may receive questions from potential bidders via the eBay site, perhaps on the exact condition of an item on offer, how old it is and what it originally cost. Making sure that you respond quickly increases your chance of a sale and will help to boost a potential buyer's confidence in you.

Your rights

Since eBay only facilitates transactions, it is not responsible for them. If you're having problems with something you've bought, your first port of call is to contact the seller via the website.

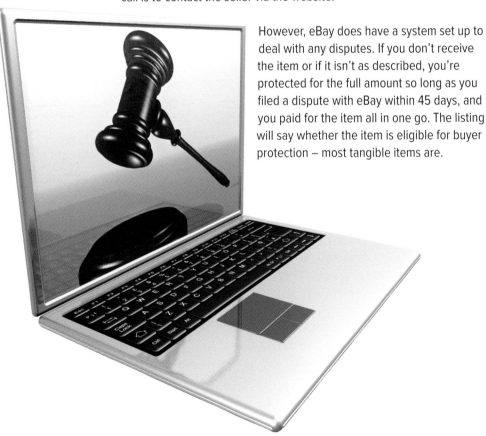

However, eBay does have a system set up to deal with any disputes. If you don't receive the item or if it isn't as described, you're protected for the full amount so long as you filed a dispute with eBay within 45 days, and you paid for the item all in one go. The listing will say whether the item is eligible for buyer protection – most tangible items are.

USE PAYPAL

Unless you're selling a car or property, you're required to offer PayPal as a method of payment (www.paypal.co.uk) on eBay. PayPal is the electronic payment system, which eBay owns. PayPal transfers funds between buyers and sellers and gives you a secure online account that stores your credit card or bank account details, but won't reveal these details to the person you're buying from or selling to.

The majority of eBay transactions are with PayPal as most buyers are likely to want to pay using it. That way they're usually protected for the full amount (see Your rights, opposite). Each listing will say whether the item is eligible for buyer protection; most tangible items are. PayPal is also fast and free for buyers. As a seller you'll be charged a small transaction fee. After eBay's taken its cut, your received funds are transferred into your PayPal account, from where you can withdraw it into your bank account or credit it to your card.

To set up a PayPal account:

1 Go to www. paypal.com

2 Click **Sign up**

3 Select your country from the drop-down list

4 Click **Get Started** under the Personal section

5 Enter your details on the form that appears

6 Click **Agree** and **Create Account**

7 You can now log into your account and manage your transactions

▶ Online Activities

TRY THIS
You can use price comparison websites to find out where to buy items for the cheapest price. Popular sites include PriceRunner (www.pricerunner.co.uk) and Kelkoo (www.kelkoo.co.uk).

SHOP SAFELY ONLINE

Internet shopping means there's no queuing and, because it's easier to shop around, often you'll save money, too.

Before you buy

Ensure you have a firewall switched on and anti-virus and anti-spyware software installed (see page 198 for more on security).

Choose a reputable retailer such as a familiar high-street store, or use an online directory such as www.safebuy.org.uk or www.shopsafe.co.uk that lists only shops offering secure credit card transactions, with obvious delivery prices and clear returns policies.

On the site

▶ If you want to buy something, you'll usually need to register first. This generally involves setting up a user name and password and entering your contact and delivery details

▶ Secure web addresses start with the letters https, instead of http, and you should see a padlock symbol at the top of the page

▶ Find out how easy the website is to contact. Look for links called **Contact us** or **Help** to find the physical address and phone number. Call to make sure the line's working and that someone picks up. If there's only an email address, send one to see how quickly they reply

▶ Investigate the small print/terms and conditions. How much does delivery cost? Are goods in stock? Can you send items back if they're not what you expected?

▶ Ensure you keep a record of the transaction and the order number. You should receive a receipt via email; if you have spam-filtering software, this email may end up in your junk folder so do check it

Internet payments

If you use a credit card to pay for goods worth more than £100 (and up to £30,000), your card company is jointly liable with the company that you buy from for any problems. For smaller purchases, an e-cash system such as PayPal (www.paypal.co.uk – see page 101) is often used. These systems allow you to send or receive payments securely over the web without sharing your financial details or credit card number with anyone else.

Buy an item

1 Click the button marked **Add to shopping basket**

2 Many websites allow you to **View basket** so you can check what you've added, the total cost, and how many of each item you've ordered. Then you can either shop some more or make your payment

3 To pay, click the **Proceed to checkout** button (or equivalent). Be aware that many online retailers will only deliver goods to the billing address of your credit card. If you haven't already registered, you'll be asked to

4 Now you can enter your payment details and purchase your item

Your rights when buying online

If you buy online from a UK or EU-based company you have the same rights as if you'd bought from a shop. Goods must be of satisfactory quality, fit for purpose and as described when sold. If a retailer breaches any of these terms, you have a right to reject the goods within a reasonable time and get a full refund. Or you can demand that the retailer repairs or replaces the item. If you send goods back for any reason that is the fault of the supplier, you should not have to pay the postage.

Cooling-off period

If you change your mind about the goods, or they don't arrive on time, the Distance Selling Regulations (DSR) give you a cooling-off period. This starts from the moment you place the order and ends seven working days from the day after you receive the goods. During this period you can cancel without having to give a reason. Contact the seller and quote the Distance Selling Regulations to get a refund and arrange to send back the purchase. These regulations don't apply to items bought from foreign websites or to items such as unsealed CDs/DVDs.

TIP

Amazon (www.amazon.co.uk) is a popular site for buying books, DVDs, etc.

▶ Online Activities

WATCH A YOUTUBE CLIP

YouTube (www.youtube.com) is a video-sharing website that lets you search for and view video clips added by members.

You can search on the site and watch clips without logging in, but, by creating an account, you can add comments about video clips that you have viewed, bookmark your favourites and give them star ratings out of five. You can even post your own creations to the site.

Search for a clip

1 Type www.youtube.com into the address bar of your web browser

2 Whenever a video is posted to YouTube, its author assigns search terms (key words) to it that help other people find it. In the search box type in a few key words that describe what you're looking for. If you want to look at some videos of koalas, for example, try Cute Koalas. Click **Search**

3 You'll be shown a list of results that match your search

4 To watch a video clip, click on a video link and it should start playing automatically

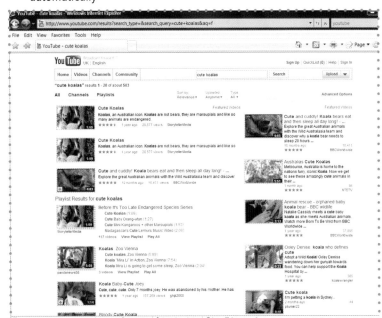

TRY THIS

Can't hear any sound with the clip you're watching? Your computer's sound might be turned down or muted – check the volume by clicking on the speaker icon in the system tray (bottom right of your screen).

5 Click the Pause symbol to pause the clip and the Play symbol to resume play. Adjust volume by clicking on the speaker icon and using the slider bar

The Sneezing baby panda

0:03 / 0:16

★★★★★ 2,784 ratings   1,514,870 views

Favourite   ➔ Share   Playlists   Flag

Bebo   MySpace

Full screen

Play/Pause

Volume

6 You may have to wait for the clip to load before you can watch it. This is illustrated by the red bar filling up. You can view a later part of the clip by clicking on the corresponding part of the red bar

7 To blow up the clip so it can be viewed larger in 'full screen' mode, click the button at the bottom right corner of the video. Press **Esc** to return to small screen mode

8 Rather than search for a specific clip, you can also browse what's popular. Click the **Videos** tab on the YouTube home page and choose a subject on the left, such as Pets & Animals

9 Under **Most Viewed** you can see what video clips have been the most popular that day

NEXT STEP ⊙

Once you've set up a YouTube account you can post your own video by clicking on the **Upload** button (top right of the screen) and following the onscreen instructions.

▶ Online Activities

SOCIAL NETWORKING EXPLAINED

Social networking brings a whole new dimension to the way that you interact with people online. Sites like Facebook and MySpace enable you to join an online group where you can:

- ▶ Email messages to friends

- ▶ Leave messages, pictures and graphics on friends' message boards – a kind of online 'pin board'

- ▶ Share photographs

- ▶ Share video clips

- ▶ Download applets – small programs that perform specific tasks. These enable you to play games like Scrabble or Chess, or take quizzes

Who is in these social networks?

People of all ages now use social networking sites. Your initial contact on the site is likely to be with friends and family, people with whom you already have something in common. Once you're established on a site you may wish to make friends with new people – perhaps those with whom you share an interest or who live in your area.

Which social network site should I join?

If you happen to know that loads of your friends are already using a particular service, that alone might be enough to make you sign up. But, if you're joining to meet new people, or to find people with common interests, you might want to look for a site that's targeted at a particular demographic. For example Saga Zone (www.sagazone.co.uk) is aimed at people over fifty.

How do I access a social network?

You access your social networking site via a web browser in the same way that you'd visit any website. You don't need new specialist software to use these sites, although you'll find that some of them do encourage you to download new applications or particular software.

How do I join?

1 Go to the home page of the social networking site you want to join

2 Click on **Sign up** or **Register** (this will differ depending on the site)

Sign Up
It's free and anyone can join

3 You'll need to enter some personal details to get started.
The policies on what information and how much tend to vary from website to website

4 Once you've filled in your details, a confirmation email will usually be sent. Click on the link in the email to activate your account

5 Now you can find friends and add information to your profile

Is it easy to find my friends?

A friend may invite you (often via email) to join a social networking group to which they already belong, in which case they've already found you. Some social networking websites will search their sites for people listed in your email address book and let you know whether they're members of the site. In other cases you may need to search for a friend's name by manually entering it into a search box on the site.

What's an online profile?

Many social networking sites allow you to enter a 'profile'. This is where people can find out information about you: your name, location, photo and your interests. You don't have to enter it, but sharing this information means others can see whether they're likely to hit it off with you.

What about security?

When you put personal details on the internet, you must think about where they'll end up. If things go wrong (the site you're signed up with has a computer security breach, for example) your information may end up in the wrong hands. The sites do work hard to prevent this, but don't enter personal details such as your date of birth, phone number or address.

BE CAREFUL

Most social networking sites enable you to choose whether your profile is public or private (look for **Privacy settings** or a similar title). This affects who can view your profile and send you messages.

▶ Online Activities

LISTEN TO MUSIC ONLINE

As well as downloading music (see page 175) you can listen to music directly over a broadband internet connection. This means no music files are permanently stored on your computer. Although you have to to be connected to the internet to listen, the plus side is that it's available to play almost immediately.

Spotify is an online music streaming service, that is both legal and free – the artists are paid royalties for the music you listen to. Major record labels have signed up to allow Spotify to distribute their catalogues, including Universal, EMI, Warner Music and AMG. Bear in mind that you will have to listen to occasional adverts, though (unless you pay to upgrade your account). Here's how to use the website.

GET STARTED WITH SPOTIFY

1 Go to www.spotify.com

2 Click **Download**

3 Enter your details to register your account. Click **Create account**

4 Instructions will appear on how to download the Spotify software

5 Click **Download Now**

6 A window will appear requesting to start the download. Click **Run**

7 Wait while Spotify downloads. A green bar will show you its progress and the length of time it will still take. Another window will then appear asking where you want to install Spotify. Click **Install** and Spotify will be saved in your Programs folder by default

8 Once installation is complete, you can log into your account

9 When you first start Spotify the Home screen appears, showing album covers of the latest music available, including popular new releases. Clicking on an album cover immediately brings up the track listing for that album (for more on creating playlists, see below)

FIND AND PLAY YOUR MUSIC

One of the main functions of Spotify is creating your own personal playlists containing only the tracks you want to hear.

1 When logged in to your Spotify account, type your chosen music – artist, song title, album name or genre – into the search bar

2 Click **Enter**

3 Advanced searches are also possible by entering something such as 'Tina Turner year:1970-1980', for example

4 The main panel then displays the music search results, consisting of artist and album suggestions, plus a track listing of all the music that meets your search criteria

5 Double click on any track and it will start playing

6 Right click on a track and you can select **Save to** if you want to save a track to a playlist (this only saves the track to your Spotify account rather than to your computer). **Queue** will line it up next in your playlist

TIP
To download music to put on your iPod or MP3 player, see page 175.

▶ Online Activities

SET UP AN ONLINE BANK ACCOUNT

You can set up an online account using your existing bank account, or open a brand new internet-only account.

With your own bank

1 Type the address of your bank's website into the address bar. You'll find the website address on your bank statement or other literature your bank may have sent you

2 On the bank's home page click on Register underneath the heading for internet banking

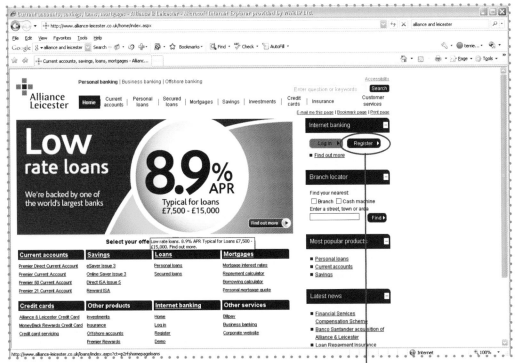

3 You'll need your sort code and account number at hand. Type them in when prompted, along with your personal details (likely to include your name, address and date of birth). You may also need a User ID or specific login details – contact your bank to check

TRY THIS

Many banks offer free security software or a subscription for a certain period when you sign up. Always check the terms and conditions before you subscribe to anything. For more on securing your computer, see page 199.

4 Once your account is set up, and if you're sure that your PC and internet connection are secure (see page 199), you can now log on to your account. If you lose or forget your password, you should phone your bank

5 Always remember to log out of your account when you're finished

With another bank

1 If you want to set up a brand new account online, enter that bank's website address in the address bar, go to the current account section, click on your desired account and fill in the form that appears

2 You'll usually get a decision on whether your application has been successful within a couple of minutes

3 As above, ensure that your PC and internet connection are secure before logging on to your account

BE CAREFUL

Fraudsters frequently rely on people using poorly chosen passwords such as 'password' or a sequence of letters or repeated numbers. To make sure you have a strong password use a mixture of numbers and upper and lower case letters, and don't use the same one that you use for other accounts, like your email, for example.

▶ Online Activities

BANK ACCOUNT SAFETY TIPS

▶ Only log on to your online bank account if you know you're using a secure PC. Avoid using public computers, including those in your office, as you can't be sure of how secure they are

▶ Secure sites will be prefixed with https:// (rather than http://) and a padlock will appear by the website address

▶ If possible, memorise your password rather than writing it down. Don't give your password to anyone, and never give your full password over the phone or email. Your bank will never ask for your whole password, they will only ask for certain digits, for example, the first and fourth numbers in your password, so beware of anyone who does

▶ Make sure your security software is up to date, and secure your wireless network (see page 77)

▶ Only access your account by using the website address provided by the bank. This means you can be certain that you are on the correct (safe and secure) website when you enter your details. If you search for your bank's site using a search engine (see page 86), you could end up on a site set up by fraudsters to illegally obtain your bank details

▶ **Never** follow a link from an email claiming to be from your bank

Jargon buster

Phishing
A type of email scam where you're tricked into giving away personal details on a spoof website that resembles the site of an official organisation (a bank, for example).

STAYING IN TOUCH

By reading and following all the steps in this chapter, you will get to grips with:

- ▷ **Sending emails**

- ▷ **Dealing with spam**

- ▷ **Chatting online using a webcam**

▶ Staying in Touch

EMAIL

An email account allows you to send and receive messages. You can also store emails that you want to keep, and create an address book with important information like phone numbers and both mailing and email addresses. To send emails, you can either use an email client like Outlook Express or Windows Mail, or a webmail account.

An email client is simply the email program where emails are stored on your computer. With these, many email activities (reading received messages, writing messages, etc.) can be done when you're not online, but to send and receive emails you need to be connected to the internet.

Webmail accounts can only be accessed when you're connected to the internet, but the benefit is that you can access all of your emails from any computer with the internet, rather than just from your home computer.

USE WINDOWS LIVE MAIL

There are a number of webmail accounts to choose from, including Google's Gmail (www.gmail.com), Yahoo! Mail (https://login.yahoo.com) and Windows Live Mail (home.live.com – this was previously Hotmail).

Create a Windows Live Mail Account

The first thing you'll need to do is set up a Windows Live ID, which will give you access to a personalised home page as well as a Windows Live Mail account.

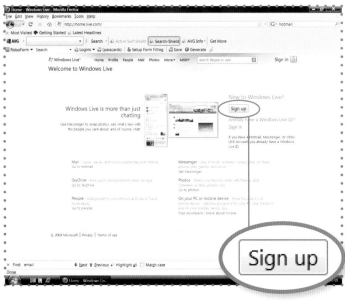

1 Go to http://home.live. com. Click on the **Sign up** button

2 Enter a Windows Live ID (usually a version of your name) and click **Check availability**. If your preferred ID isn't available, Windows Live will suggest alternatives. For example, if JohnSmith isn't available, you may be offered JohnSmith342

3 Choose a password for your account. Either then enter an alternative email address (if you have one) so that Windows Live Mail can send you a reminder of your password if needed, or click **Or choose a security question for password reset**. Click the drop-down arrow and choose a reminder question

4 Enter your personal details and copy the series of characters at the bottom of the screen. Click **I accept**

5 To make changes to your profile (this contains information such as contact information), click **Profile**

6 Click **Edit profile details**

7 Click the relevant buttons to add a picture, enter your age, contact information, etc. Don't add any sensitive information

8 The default setting on Windows Live Mail is to share your profile information publicly i.e. with anyone who has a Windows Live account. To change this, click on the link that currently reads **Everyone (public)** under **Contact info.** Untick the box that says **Everyone (public)**

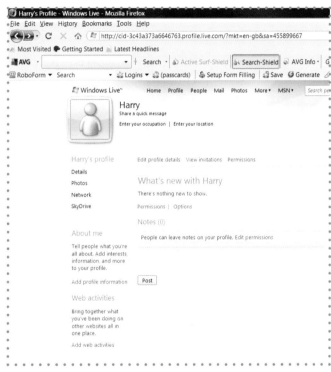

9 Tick the box that reads **My network**, which means your information is only accessible to those in your contact list, not to others. Click **Save**

Staying in Touch

Send an email

Once you've set up your webmail account, you'll want to send emails. Find out the email addresses of some family and friends and you're ready to get started.

1 Go to home.live.com. Log into your Windows Live Mail account with your Windows Live ID and password

2 On the homepage click **Mail** to access your Windows Live Mail (alternatively you can bookmark http://mail.live.com to go straight to your email account – see page 92 for more on bookmarking).

3 To send an email click **New**

4 Type the email address of the recipient in the **To** box (for example, JohnSmith@hotmail.com) or click on **To**: to reveal any friends' addresses you have added to your **Contacts**

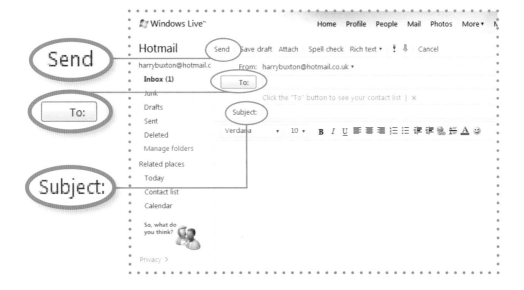

5 Enter a subject line for your email and type your text

6 Click **Send**

Filter emails

To filter emails from family members or a specific group of friends so that they automatically go into one folder, you'll need to set up a new folder.

1 Click **Manage Folders**

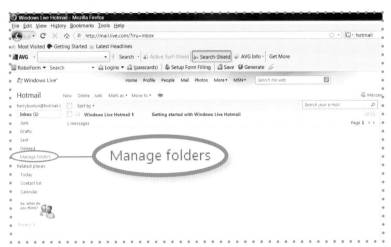

2 Click **New** and give your folder a name (for example, 'Family')

3 Press **Enter**

4 Click **Options** (on the right-hand side of the screen), then **More Options**

5 Under **Customize your email**, click **Automatically sort e-mail into folders**

6 Click **New Filter**

7 Select **From address** and **Contains** from drop-down menus (if they aren't already seclected) and enter the email address of a family member (you can only enter one address at a time)

8 Put a dot next to the new 'Family' folder you created in step 2

9 Click **Save**. The emails from that person will now automatically go to that folder

BE CAREFUL

If you've set up a filter, remember to check the new folder you've created for emails from those people.

Staying in Touch

SET UP A GMAIL ACCOUNT

1 Gmail (also known as Google Mail) is another popular webmail provider.

2 Type mail.google.com in the address bar of your browser

3 On the Google Mail home page, click **Create an account**

4 This will open a registration page asking you to fill in your details (for example, creating a login name and password). If your chosen name isn't available, you'll have to enter an alternative. Once you've done this, click **I Accept/Create my Account**

5 Once your account is created, go to the web page mail.google.com to log into your account

Send an email on Google Mail

1 Go to the web page mail.google.com to log into your account

2 Enter your username and password that you created in step 3 (opposite). Click **Sign in**

3 You can now start emailing. Click on **Compose Mail** (top left of the screen) to write an email

Send instant messages to friends on Google Mail

1 Click **Add contact** in the Chat menu on the left-hand side

2 Enter your friend's email address. Click **Send invites** to invite them to chat

3 To chat with a friend, make sure they are online (when they are also logged into Google Mail, they will have a green dot next to their name) and click on their name to open a window where you can type your messages

▶ Staying in Touch

EMAIL CLIENTS

Windows Vista PCs will come with an email client called Windows Mail (not to be confused with Windows Live Mail, which is a webmail account, see page 114). Windows Mail replaces Outlook Express, which is part of a previous versions of Windows. You may also find that your ISP (internet service provider) provides you with the option to use its email client.

Main toolbar
Buttons for the main functions, such as sending and receiving mail, creating new messages and replying to or forwarding mail.

Folders
You'll start off with an Inbox, Outbox, Sent items, Drafts and Deleted items folder, but you can also create your own unique folders, for example 'October emails' or 'Emails from John'.

Address book
Quick access to your contacts. Once into the address book, double click on a name to open a new email message to that person.

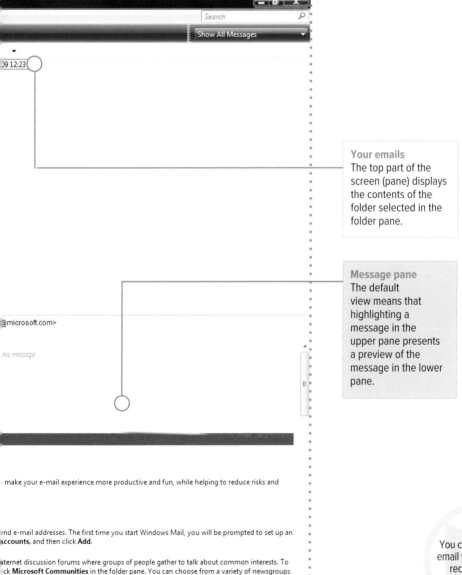

Your emails
The top part of the screen (pane) displays the contents of the folder selected in the folder pane.

Message pane
The default view means that highlighting a message in the upper pane presents a preview of the message in the lower pane.

make your e-mail experience more productive and fun, while helping to reduce risks and

nd e-mail addresses. The first time you start Windows Mail, you will be prompted to set up an ccounts, and then click **Add**.

ternet discussion forums where groups of people gather to talk about common interests. To ck **Microsoft Communities** in the folder pane. You can choose from a variety of newsgroups

TIP
You can forward an email you've already received on to another recipient (see page 127).

121

▶ Staying in Touch

SET UP A WINDOWS MAIL ACCOUNT

These instructions are split into different steps for ease, but you'll need to do them all in order to set up your account.

Get your account details

1 During the setup process you'll need to enter some details about your email account. This information should have been sent to you when you signed up with your internet service provider

2 Enter your username, password and the addresses for your ISP's incoming and outgoing email servers (as sent to you by your ISP)

3 You'll also need to know whether your service requires Secure Password Authentication, and if it uses POP3, IMAP or HTTP. You don't need to understand this jargon, you just need to get these details from your internet service provider (if they haven't sent them already) and enter them at the appropriate times during setup

Enter your name

1 Click [image] and click **All programs**

2 Click **Windows Mail**

3 The **Windows Mail setup wizard** should appear (if it doesn't, go to **Tools** and click **Accounts**)

4 Click the **Add** button and, in the window that appears, highlight the words **E-mail Account** and click **Next**. In the following screen, enter your name as you want it to appear in your emails (this can be in any form you like) and click **Next**

Enter your email address

1 Type your email address (as stipulated by your ISP)

2 Click **Next**

3 Select the server type (your ISP should give you this information) from the drop-down list at the top of the next window

4 Underneath, you'll see two boxes, for the incoming and outgoing server addresses. Enter the details provided by your ISP here

5 If required (see point 3 under 'Get your account details') tick the box that says **Outgoing server requires authentication**

6 Click **Next**

Security details

1 Enter your username and password into the boxes provided. Again, these details should have been given to you by your ISP

2 If you don't want to have to enter your password every time you check your mail, put a tick in the box next to **Remember password** and click **Next**

3 On the congratulations screen, click **Finish** to exit the wizard. You're now ready to start using Windows Mail

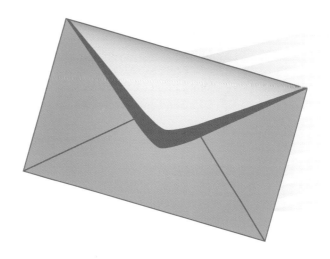

Check your emails

When you open Windows Mail, if you're connected to the internet, it will check to see if you've got any messages and download these to your inbox. Then it will check every half hour (by default) for any new messages. If you want to check in between, you can do this manually by following these steps:

1 Make sure you're connected to the internet

2 Click **Tools**

3 Select **Send and Receive**

4 Click **Send and Receive All**

5 Any new messages will arrive in your inbox

Open and read an email

1 Select **Inbox** from the folders list

2 Click once on the message you want to read and it will appear in the bottom half of the screen automatically

3 To open the message in a separate, bigger window, double click on the message

Staying in Touch

Write and send an email

1 Click **Create Mail.** A new window will appear

2 In the **To** box, type the email address of the person you're writing to. Or you can use your address book/contacts (see page 130 for more on this)

3 As well as the To field, most email programs have **CC** (carbon copy) and **BCC** (blind carbon copy) fields that allow you to copy your email to others. When you use the CC field, all recipients are aware who has received a copy of the email. The BCC field can be used if you don't want any of the recipients to know who else the email has been copied to

4 In the **Subject** box, type a title for your message

5 In the box below, type your message

6 When you're finished, click **Send**

TIP
If you can't see the **CC** and **BCC** fields then click **View** and then **All Headers.**

Reply to and forward an email

1 To reply to a message, open it and click **Reply** (top left of the screen). This will automatically open a new window (with the recipient's email address already entered) where you can write your email

2 To forward a message, open the message and click **Forward**. This will open a new window where you can write your email. You will need to enter the recipient's email address (see step 2, opposite)

Delete an email

1 In your inbox, click once on the message you want to delete

2 On the toolbar click **Edit**, then **Delete**

3 Alternatively, in the inbox, right click on the message and click **Delete**

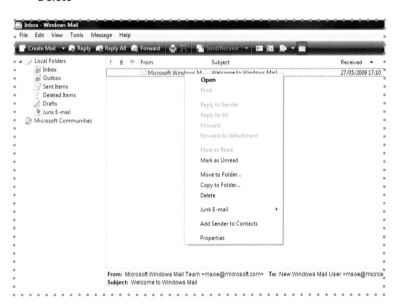

4 To select multiple messages, hold down the **Ctrl** key while you click each message you want to delete until they're all highlighted. Then follow step 2 or step 3

Attach a file to an email

Sometimes you might want to send a picture or separate document with your email. Here's how:

1 Once you've written your email click the paper clip icon

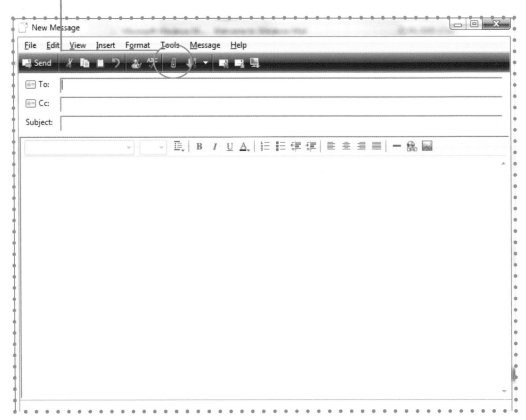

2 Locate the file you want to send and click on it (photographs are likely to be in your Pictures folder)

3 Click **Open**

BE CAREFUL

Attaching files and pictures to your emails can create unwieldy emails – if your email attachment is too big, you may see an error message that means it exceeds the email attachment limit for your account.

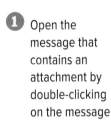 The file will appear in the **Attach** box

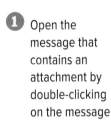 Add other attachments in the same way. Click **Send**

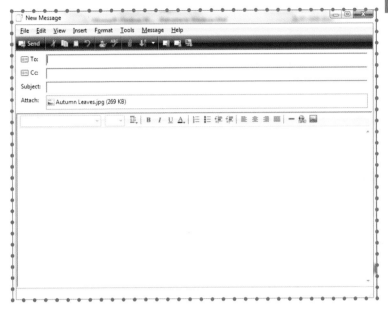

Open an attachment
If someone sends you a picture or document attached to an email, you'll need to open it.

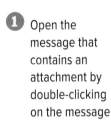 Open the message that contains an attachment by double-clicking on the message

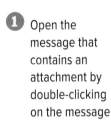 Double click on the file attachment icon at the top of the new message window

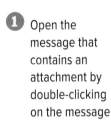 The attachment will open in a new window. Then you can save it from here (for more on saving see page 33)

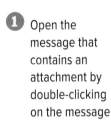 To save an attachment first before opening it, open the message as above and click **File** in the message window

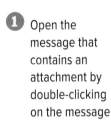 Click **Save Attachments**

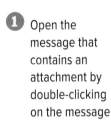 A folder list will appear. Select the folder into which you want to save the attachment

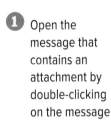 Select the attachment you want to save (if there's more than one)

 Click **Save**. Repeat for other attachments if there are any

BE CAREFUL

Only open attachments if you know the sender. Those from unknown senders could contain viruses. See page 198 for more on computer security.

129

ADD AN ADDRESS TO WINDOWS CONTACTS

Windows Contacts acts as an address book where you can store the details of people you know. Once you've added a contact you won't need to type out their email address when you use Windows Mail. Here's how to add a contact:

1 Click

2 Click **All Programs**

3 Click **Windows Contacts**

4 Click **New Contact**

5 Type the information for your contact into the relevant boxes and click **OK**

Adding a picture of your contact to Windows Contacts

1 Double click on the name of the contact, for example, Charlie Buxton

2 On the **Name and e-mail** tab, click on the dummy picture

3 Click **Change picture**

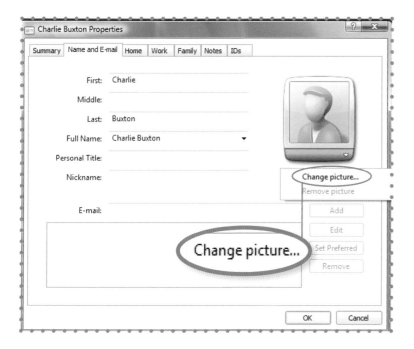

4 Choose the picture you want from your folders by clicking on it and then clicking **Set**

5 Click **OK**

6 To remove a picture, click **Remove picture** (in step 3) instead

▶ Staying in Touch

DEAL WITH SPAM

Spam is the electronic equivalent of junk mail. It can clog up your inbox with rubbish and make it hard to sift through messages. Spam emails can also contain offensive material and are often the carriers of viruses and phishing scams (see page 134).

Some internet service providers use spam filters on their email server to try to prevent this; webmail accounts usually feature spam filters too. You can also adapt your email program to filter out certain types of message automatically by changing your junk email settings.

Filter junk mail in Windows Live Mail (Hotmail)

1 Click **Options** in the top right of your screen

2 Click **More options**

3 Under **Junk Mail**, click **Filters and Reporting**

4 From the list that appears, you can select how your account deals with junk mail

5 Click **Save** at the bottom of the page when you've chosen

Filter junk mail in Windows Mail

1 Click **Tools** on the toolbar

2 Click **Junk E-mail Options**

3 A window will appear. Here you can choose the level of protection you want

4 Make your choices and click **Apply**

5 Click **OK**

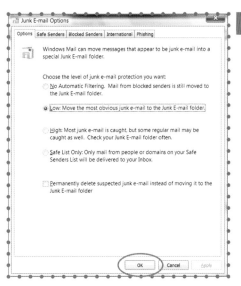

TOP TIPS FOR AVOIDING SPAM

Don't reply to spam emails
Replying to spam emails or clicking on an 'unsubscribe' link within them confirms to the sender that your email address is genuine. Simply delete them without opening.

Create a 'disposable' email address
Create a separate email to use for online shopping, forums and signing up for services – something like a free Windows Live Hotmail account (http://mail.live.com) that you can always scrap and start again.

Choose a complicated email address
Picking an obscure email address can help prevent spammers from sending anything to you.

Use a spam filter
It is best to keep the junk at bay by using a dedicated spam filter. The best of these use a white list for 'good' email addresses and a black list for addresses, keywords and phrases that you don't want in your inbox. Most email accounts include a spam filter, but there are also dedicated spam-filtering tools available, including free downloadable ones like Mailwasher (www.mailwasher.net) and SpamFighter (www.spamfighter.com).

Identify spam to your email provider
Report spam to your internet service provider or webmail service provider. This can help your provider to determine and eliminate future spam emails. Often you can do this by clicking **Report this email as junk** when prompted.

NEXT STEP

Spam emails can try to lure you into phishing scams. Read more about how to avoid these on page 134.

AVOID PHISHING SCAMS

Phishing is the name given to cons where unwitting victims are hooked into handing over personal information on email – bank account details, passwords, credit card numbers and the like – by criminals who sell this data on or make use of it themselves to commit fraud.

Phishing scams frequently take the form of a hoax spam email that looks like it came from an official source, such as your bank or building society. The email may ask you to email back personal account details, or to click on a link within the message. The link takes you to a fake website that looks like the real thing. Entering any login details, bank account numbers or any personal info into such a web page will give your sensitive data to identity thieves. The best thing to do is delete any suspicious emails and avoid any suspicious sites. However, there are also dedicated filters that can help you to spot the scams.

PHISHING FILTERS

Most web browsers have built-in tools for spotting fake sites and potentially dangerous web pages. Most phishing filters compare the site you're visiting against a list of known hoax pages, and then warn you if it looks like the web address you're visiting might be fraudulent.

Turn on the phishing filter in Internet Explorer

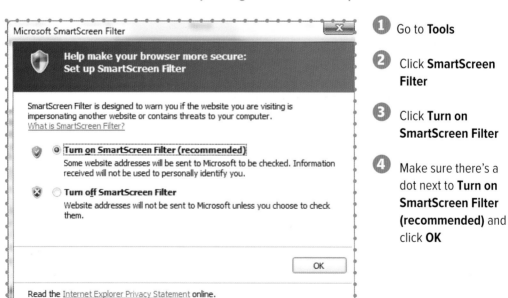

1 Go to **Tools**

2 Click **SmartScreen Filter**

3 Click **Turn on SmartScreen Filter**

4 Make sure there's a dot next to **Turn on SmartScreen Filter (recommended)** and click **OK**

Report a potential hoax website in Internet Explorer

① While on a suspect web page, click **Tools**

② Click **SmartScreen Filter**

③ Click **Report Unsafe Website**

④ A new window will open showing the address of the site. Tick next to **I think this is a phishing website**

⑤ Type the characters that you can see in the box at the bottom

⑥ Click **Submit**

Turn on the phishing filter in Firefox

① Go to **Tools**

② Click **Options**

③ Under the **Security** tab, make sure there's a tick next to where it says **Tell me if the site I'm visiting is a suspected forgery**

Report a potential hoax website in Firefox

① With the web page open, go to **Help**

② Click **Report Web Forgery**

③ This will bring up a web page where you can report the suspected site

④ Add a comment if you want to and click **Submit Report**

Report Unsafe Website

NEXT STEP

To find out more about phishing and other internet scams see page 136.

HOW TO SPOT A PHISHING SCAM

Dear Valued Customer

We recently have determined that different computers have logged into your Which? Bank account, and multiple password failures were present before the logons.

In this manner for your security, your specified access account has been locked and needs to be reactivated, in order for it to remain active, please Use the link below to proceed and unlock your account.

So we want you to use this oppurtunity to upgrade your account to our new security with the Which? Bank.

https://www.mybank.which/index.asp?

I am convinced that Which? Bank will be a leading UK bank focused on giving you great service and value-for-money products.

Yours sincerely

Chairman, Which? Bank

This message was sent to you as a Which? Bank customer, to inform you regarding important information about your account.

*This email and the use of a Which? Bank logo is for illustrative purposes only.

Logos
These might look like the real deal, but logos are easily copied and are not a guarantee of authenticity.

Impersonal
The email might be addressed to 'Dear valued customer' or 'valued client'. Your bank will not email you.

Scare tactics
To frighten you into taking action they might tell you that someone has tried to access your bank fraudulently and that you must login now to verify your personal details or your account will be closed.

Spelling/grammar
There might be spelling mistakes, poor syntax (overuse of capital letters, etc.) or wording may be overcomplicated.

Link
They will send you an emailed link to a fraudulent web page. This may look suspicious or it may be exactly the same address as the genuine login page. Never click on an emailed link.

The small print
This might look genuine but it could easily be copied from a genuine email so is not a guarantee of authenticity.

NEXT STEP

For more security threats and how to avoid them, see page 198 onwards.

Staying in Touch

EMAIL ETIQUETTE

Here are the top ten dos and don'ts when it comes to sending emails.

The dos

Do **tone it down**
Avoid the use of capital letters. Capitals are harder to read and are the email equivalent of shouting at someone, which may cause offence.

Do **respect privacy**
It's a common mistake but, when sending out a group email, try to remember to put all the email addresses in the blind carbon copy **(BCC)** field rather than the **To** or **CC** fields. That way, you'll be respecting the privacy of all the people on your recipient list by keeping their email addresses hidden from all the others.

Do **address the issue**
Double check all addresses you enter manually to make sure your email message doesn't end up going to the wrong person or being returned to you as undeliverable mail.

Do **stick to the subject**
Try to make sure the subject field of your emails contains something meaningful to help your recipient know what the email is about.

Do **spellcheck**
It's always worth using your email program's spellchecker before you hit send – particularly for more formal communications.

NEXT STEP ▶

For more advice on emails, see page 114.

The don'ts

Don't **open it**

Don't open any email attachments unless you're 100 per cent sure they are legitimate. If you recognise the name of the person sending you an email but weren't expecting an attachment, it's worth checking with them that they meant to send it to you. Some sneaky viruses can hijack people's email accounts without their knowledge.

Don't **be too forward**

Think before you forward something on to other people. If it's a joke, it might not always be appreciated. And, even if you forward something that looks like helpful advice, you could just be helping to perpetuate junk email messages. Plus, it may clog up the recipient's inbox, which could prevent them from receiving further emails if they have a limit on their email storage.

Don't **overdo it**

You can cheer up your emails with fonts, colours and graphics, but don't go overboard. Less is more, where email is concerned – not everyone's email program will be able to display your formatting anyway.

Don't **get too personal**

Never include any sensitive personal data in your email messages. Email is not a particularly secure method of communication and therefore not suitable for things like bank details, credit card numbers, passwords, etc.

Don't **get too attached**

Keep an eye on the size (in KB or MB) of the files you send. Big attachments can be a pain for the person you send them to, as they take much longer to download. A large attachment could clog up the recipient's mailbox and, if the person you're sending it to uses a pay-as-you-go internet service, it might even cost them more money.

EMAIL PICTURES

Digital cameras can generate extremely large image files that may clog up another person's inbox if you attach them to an email straight after you've transferred them to your computer. The large size of an image might also mean it gets sent straight to the recipient's junk mail folder or be blocked altogether. Or, even if they can view the picture, it may be so large that they have to scroll up, down and across to see the whole image.

Fortunately, Windows Vista features a handy tool that allows you to resize pictures for easy sending. This involves altering their resolution. When emailing a picture, consider what the person receiving it wants to do with it before choosing an image size (see point 6).

1 Click

2 Click **Control Panel**

3 Click **Windows Photo Gallery**

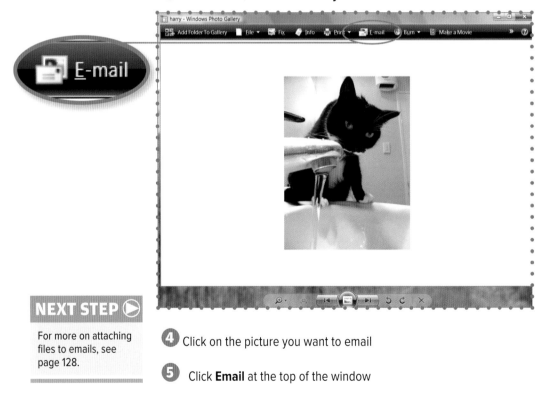

NEXT STEP ⊳

For more on attaching files to emails, see page 128.

4 Click on the picture you want to email

5 Click **Email** at the top of the window

6 Choose the picture size you want from the drop-down menu. The 'smaller' size is fine if the recipient will only be looking at the photos on screen, while 'small' is suitable for printing photos sized 4 x 6 inches. Both 'medium' and 'large' are suitable for printing photos sized 5 x 7 inches

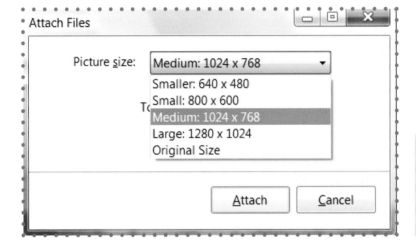

TRY THIS

In many email programs you can right click on an attachment and click **Properties** to see more information about it (including size and file type).

7 Once you've selected the dimensions, you'll see the estimated size of your attachment. Anything less than 1MB is fine to send via email

8 If it's OK, click **Attach**

NEXT STEP ▶

You don't have to email photos to share them with a friend – you can post them on a photo-sharing website and invite friends to view them. See page 156.

MAKE PHONE CALLS ONLINE

Making phone calls over the internet is often referred to as VoIP (Voice over Internet Protocol). VoIP phone calls are generally cheaper than standard landline or mobile phone calls, and in some cases are completely free. As long as you have a basic microphone headset, you can make and receive calls with VoIP services like Skype without buying any extra expensive hardware, though you can buy a dedicated Skype handset (similar to a traditional phone) if you don't want to use a headset.

TRY THIS

If a warning appears when you try to download Skype, check at the top of the window. Your web browser may be blocking the download. Click on the warning bar and click **Download file**.

Download and install Skype

1 Open your web browser and type www.skype.com/intl/en-gb into the address bar. Press **Enter**

2 Click **Download Skype**

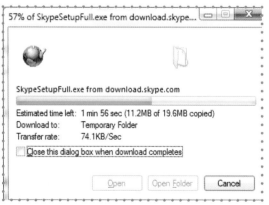

3 When the File Download dialogue box appears, click **Run**

4 Click **I agree – install**. A window will appear showing the progress of the download

5 Once the file has downloaded, click **Finish**

Create an account

1 Once you've finished installing the software, there will be a **Thank You** screen. Click **Start Skype**

2 In the **Create Account** window that opens, enter your name and choose a Skype name and password

3 Check the tick box and click **Next**

4 Fill out your email address on the next screen and enter your Country/Region and your nearest city

5 Finally, check or uncheck the boxes as required and click **Sign In**

Set up

1 When you first sign into Skype, the **Getting Started** wizard will launch. Connect your headset or handset if you're using one

2 If you're using a standard microphone headset, you should find it has two plugs attached to it. Insert the pink or red one into your computer's microphone socket (this should also be pink/red or marked with the icon of a microphone)

3 Plug the green one into the headphone output (also green or marked with a stereo sound waves icon)

Make a test call

1 You'll find a Skype Test Call contact listed in your Skype contacts. To make your test call, click the green Call button next to this contact

2 Instructions should prompt you to record a message after the beep

3 You should then be able to hear the message you recorded. If you can't, onscreen instructions will tell you what to do (you may need a headset if you don't have one already)

> **TIP**
> Phone calls between Skype users are free, regardless of where in the world you're phoning.

▶ Chat Online

Add contacts

1 Ask your friends to send you their Skype names. You can then add them to your Skype contacts by clicking the **New** button

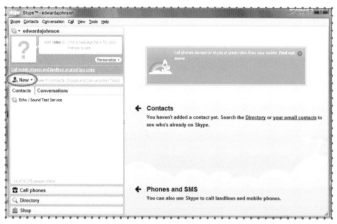

2 Click **New Contact** and enter their Skype name

3 Alternatively, you can search for people using their email address or full name. Enter the name and click **Find**

4 Select people from the list that appears and click **Add Contact**

5 Click **Close** when you're done

Make a Skype call

1 Double click on the icon on your desktop or in the system tray. Select the Contacts tab in the main Skype window and find the name of the person you want to call

2 Click on their Skype name and then click the green **Call** button

3 If they aren't listed, type their Skype name (you'll need to get this from the person you want to contact) into the box towards the top of the Skype window and click **Search Directory**

4 When you receive a call, a window will pop up asking whether you want to accept or reject it. You must be logged in to Skype to receive a call

NEXT STEP ▶

You can call a landline or mobile using your Skype account, but you'll need to buy Skype credits. Go to **Account** and click **Buy Skype Credit**. A wizard will launch that will take you through the process. Then, to make a call, click on the **Call Phones** tab in the main Skype window.

SET UP A WEBCAM

Webcams send moving images of you to another webcam-equipped computer via the internet. It's an effective way to stay in touch with friends and loved ones. Both you and the person you're talking to will need a webcam and a broadband connection. If you have a new PC/laptop it may have an integrated webcam in the screen, if not you'll need to invest in a separate webcam, which will attach to your monitor.

1 Run the set-up CD included with the webcam. This will install the drivers that the webcam needs to work with your computer (see page 81 for more on installing devices and drivers)

2 Cameras clip or rest on top of your PC. Refer to your webcam manual for specific instructions

3 Place your webcam at around eye level, and an arm's length from your face to ensure that people aren't squinting to see you or staring up your nose

4 When prompted, plug the webcam into a USB port on your computer. Windows Vista should recognise it and the software will set up the webcam's camera and the built-in microphone

5 Most webcam software provides shortcuts to the popular instant messaging services Windows Live Messenger and Skype, and often links to Yahoo! Messenger and AOL's AIM too

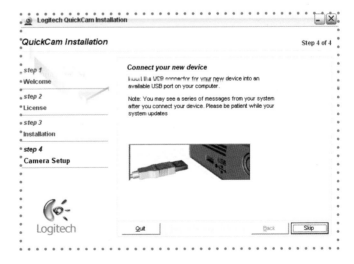

VIDEO CHAT

To talk face-to-face with distant friends via your PC and your webcam, you need to install the right software. These programs let you exchange text, sound and video messages with other users.

There's a wide choice of free video chat software available but, if you know your friends and family video chat already, check which software they use because you'll need to use the same software as them. You can also use Skype to video chat (follow the onscreen instructions once you've set up your account as on page 143). The following steps show you how to video chat using Windows Live Messenger.

Download Windows Live Messenger

1 Download the Windows Live Messenger program from get.live.com/messenger/overview

2 Click **Get it free** and follow the steps

3 Click **Run** to start Windows Live Installer (it will take a few minutes)

4 Once it's installed, a Windows Live Messenger window will pop up on your desktop. This is the window you'll see each time you log in

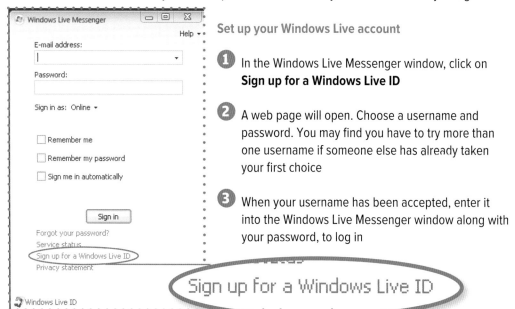

Set up your Windows Live account

1 In the Windows Live Messenger window, click on **Sign up for a Windows Live ID**

2 A web page will open. Choose a username and password. You may find you have to try more than one username if someone else has already taken your first choice

3 When your username has been accepted, enter it into the Windows Live Messenger window along with your password, to log in

Configure Windows Live Messenger

1 Windows Live Messenger will run automatically every time you start Windows. If you don't want it to, click **Tools** on the menu bar at the top of the Messenger window

2 Click **Options**

3 Click **Sign In** on the left-hand side and untick **Automatically run Windows Live Messenger when I log on to Windows**

4 Click **OK**

TIP
Open Messenger at any time by double-clicking on the Messenger icon in the taskbar.

Set up your webcam with Windows Live Messenger
Make sure the sound output (PC speakers or headphones), sound input (microphone in the webcam) and the video input (the webcam) are all working. Onscreen instructions will help if you're having problems.

1 Click **Tools**, as in step 1 above

2 Click **Audio and video setup**

3 Follow the instructions onscreen. You'll then be prompted to speak to make sure the microphone is picking up your voice

4 You'll see the image that your webcam is seeing. This should be you! Adjust the position of the webcam until you're centred. When you're happy, click **Finish**

Audio and Video Setup

Step 3: Webcam Setup

Select the webcam you would like to use:

Logitech QuickCam Pro 9000

Adjust the angle and focus of your webcam to make sure the image to the left is what you want.

Options...

< Back   Finish   Cancel

Chat Online

Find your friends

1 To find someone else using the same program, click the icon in the Windows Live Messenger menu bar. Enter your friend's instant messaging address (the same as their email address)

2 Click **Add contact**

3 A request will be sent to them. When they accept, they'll appear in your list. If they're online at the time, it may take only seconds

Make a call

TRY THIS
You can also send written messages. Double click on your friend's name and type your message in the window that appears. Every time you press **Enter** your words will appear immediately on their screen.

1 Agree with your friend when you'll be online. In the Windows Live Messenger window, right click on your friend's name

2 Click **Video** and then **Start a video call** to let them know you want to chat

3 When they click **Accept**, you should see each other

MEDIA & CREATIVITY

By reading and following all the steps in this chapter, you will get to grips with:

▶ **Organising your digital photos**

▶ **Editing video clips**

▶ **Downloading music**

TRANSFER PICTURES FROM A DIGITAL CAMERA TO A COMPUTER

Digital cameras have not only made it easier to take pictures, but also to store and circulate them electronically via your PC. Follow these instructions to transfer your pictures from a digital camera to your computer.

1 Connect the camera to your PC using a USB cable or, if your PC has a compatible card slot, you can pop the card from your camera straight into your PC. Check the camera's instruction booklet if you need help

2 A window will appear asking what you want to do next. Click **Import pictures using Windows**

3 Windows will save the photos from the memory card into your Pictures folder

4 You'll be given the option to tag your pictures as you import them. Tags are keywords that you can use to identify photos (for example, you can search for all the photos that you've tagged with 'beach' or a specific person's name). The tags you enter will apply to all the imported photos, so keep them fairly general. More specific tags can be added later on

5 Click **Import** when you're done

6 Windows Photo Gallery will open automatically to show your pictures

Transfer pictures using a scanner

Don't worry if you have non-digital photos. Some printers also allow you to scan pictures and documents. Once you've scanned something, you then have an electronic copy that you can send via email or store on your computer.

1 Place the photo on the scanner, ensuring the scanner is connected to your PC. Open Windows Photo Gallery (see page 152)

2 Click **File**

3 Click **Import from Camera or Scanner** in the drop-down menu

4 Double click on the icon that represents your scanner

5 Your scanner will scan the photo

Transfer pictures from another folder

You may have pictures in another folder that you want to move to Windows Photo Gallery. Follow these steps to transfer them:

1 In Windows Photo Gallery (see page 152 for how to open), click **File**

2 Click **Add folder to Gallery**

3 Find the folder you want to add

4 Click **OK** and then **OK** again

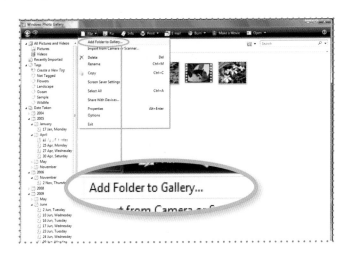

Photos

SAVE AND ORGANISE PHOTOS

Once you have your photos on your computer, you'll need to sort and manage them. You can use the Windows Photo Gallery to help you organise your pictures.

View and tag your photos

1 Click

2 Click **All Programs**

3 Click **Photo Gallery**

4 Double click on a picture to see a bigger version. From here you can browse through your pictures by clicking the left and right arrows, or you can view a slideshow (your photos automatically shown onscreen in succession without you having to click each time, allowing you to view them as if you were flicking through a photo album)

TIP

Windows Photo Gallery allows you to email photos directly from within the program (see page 140).

TRY THIS

There are other free photo-organising tools available, such as Google's Picasa and Adobe Photoshop Album Starter Edition. Both are available online.

Previous picture   Next picture

Begin slideshow

⑤ To tag a picture, double click the photo in the main window and click **Info** on the top toolbar

⑥ Click **Add tags**. If your photo has more than one tag, separate each word with a forward slash (/)

Change how your photos are listed

Windows Photo Gallery automatically organises all your photos by date. You can, however, opt to view your images by other criteria using the filters on the left-hand side of the window. For example:

NEXT STEP

You can use Photo Gallery to edit your photos, as well as print, email or burn CDs of your favourites (see page 159 for more on creating a CD of your photos).

① Click on **Date Taken** and select a year to see all the photos from that year

② If you have tagged and rated your pictures you can also click on the relevant filter on the left to view photos by the tagged keyword or rating

Photos

EDIT YOUR PHOTOS

Once you've added your photos to the Windows Photo Gallery you can use a number of editing tools to improve your pictures. In each case, follow step 1 below, and then choose what you want to do to your picture. For example, you can remove red eye or crop part of a picture.

1 Double click on the image you want to edit and click **Fix** on the main toolbar. You will see a number of options: Auto Adjust, Exposure, Colour, Crop and Fix Red Eye

2 To remove red-eye click on **Fix Red Eye**, then use the mouse pointer to drag a small rectangle around the eye you want to fix. Repeat as necessary. Remember to save a copy of your edited photo

3 To remove part of a picture, click **Crop picture**

4 A frame will appear on the picture. What's inside the frame represents the part of your picture you will retain when you crop it. Drag the edges of the frame to adjust it

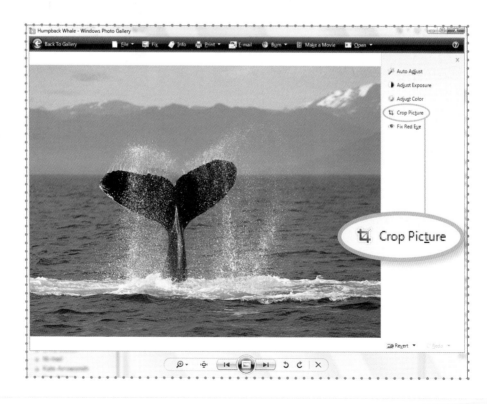

5 Click **Apply**

6 You'll see the new cropped version of your picture

7 Click **Undo** if you're not happy with the result. Or save a copy of your new picture if you are

photos

155

Photos

USE A PHOTO-SHARING SITE

Rather than emailing specific pictures, you can post your photographs online, from where friends and family (with details of the site) can see them. This allows more people to see them without filling up anyone's email system. Follow these steps to post pictures on Flickr, a popular photo-sharing website.

Create a Flickr account

1 You need a Yahoo! Account to use Flickr. To create one, go to the Flickr website www.flickr.com and click **Create Your Account**

TRY THIS

You can assign key words to your images according to the subject (a process known as tagging) and make your images easy to find in a search. You can even plot where your photos were taken on a map (called geotagging) and organise images by putting them into folders known as 'Sets'.

2 This takes you to the Yahoo! sign-up page. Click **Sign Up** (on the bottom right-hand side of the page). Enter your personal details then click **Create My Account**

3 Back on www.flickr.com, log in to Flickr using your Yahoo! account details

4 Select a screen name and click on **Create a new account**

156

Upload photographs

1 On the welcome screen click **Upload your first photos** (whenever you return to the site from now on, just click **Upload Photos and Videos** in the top right of the screen) once you've logged in

2 Select **Choose photos and videos**. This will open a window that will enable you to browse your computer for your photos

3 Select a photograph and click **Open**

4 Your photo will appear on the Flickr web page

5 Select whether you want this picture to be private, whether you want your friends and family to be able to view it, or whether to make it public and allow all Flickr users to see it

6 Click **Upload Photos and Videos**

TIP

When you log in to Flickr, click **Your Photostream** on the main page to see your pictures.

7 Add a brief description of the photo and any tags (see page 153 for more on tagging) by clicking on **Add a description**

8 Once you've done this click **Save** or, if you've uploaded more than one photo, **Save this batch**

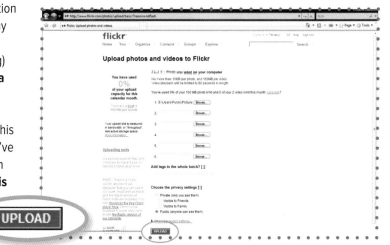

Photos

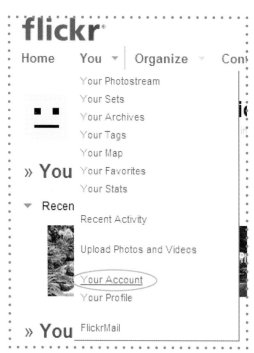

Allow others to see your photos

Once you've uploaded your photos, you can set up your own Flickr web address that you can give to friends who want to look at them.

1 When you're logged in on the Flickr website, click on the arrow next to **You** in the menu bar at the top

2 Click **Your Account**

3 Click **Create your own memorable Flickr web address!**

4 Complete your web address (make this up yourself) in the box that appears. Click **Preview**

5 Make sure that it's correct. Click **OK – Lock it in**

6 Now you can give your new address to friends to view your photos

TRY THIS

To put your pictures into a set (a folder where you can group certain photos, such as from one specific occasion), click **Organize.** Drag the photos you want to combine into a set into the grey space above. When ready, click **Add to Set**. Fill in a title and description and click **Save**.

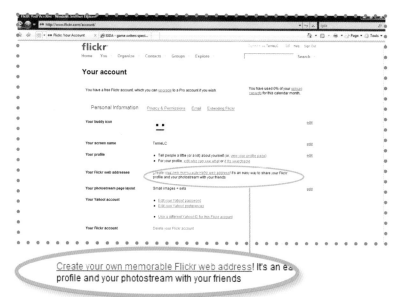

COPY YOUR PICTURES TO A CD

Once you've organised and edited your photos on your computer, you may want to save them onto a CD to share with friends or so that you have a backup copy.

① Insert a blank CD into your computer

② Click

③ Click **All Programs**

④ Click **Windows Photo Gallery**. Choose the photos you want to save by holding down the **Ctrl** button on your keyboard and single-clicking on each one in the main Gallery window

⑤ Once you have selected all the photos you want on that CD, click the **Burn** button on the top toolbar

⑥ Click **Data disc**

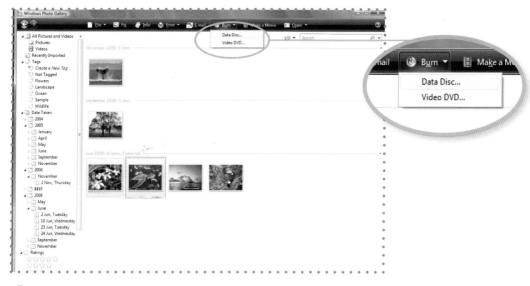

⑦ Click **Next**

⑧ Click **Yes**

photos

TRANSFER VIDEO FOOTAGE ON TO YOUR PC

A camcorder is great for capturing precious memories, whether it's a golden wedding anniversary or a special holiday. Sometimes, however, your footage may be too long, or include sections you'd rather cut.

To edit your video, you'll first need to transfer all your footage on to your computer. In some cases you may be required to use the software provided with your camcorder to do this. Alternatively, you can use Windows Movie Maker, free video-editing software that comes with Vista:

1 Connect your camcorder to your computer using a Firewire cable

2 Turn on the camcorder and set it to playback mode

3 When prompted, click **Capture Video using Windows Movie Maker**

TIP

Nearly all digital cameras now allow you to record video clips. Upload these like your photos.

TRY THIS

Video consumes more storage space than any other type of media file. Therefore, while not essential, it's preferable to store it on a separate hard drive (for more on this see page 185) if you plan on editing a lot of material.

4 Click **OK** and the Video Capture wizard will start

5 On the **Captured Video File** page, type a name for your video

6 Click **Next**

7 On the **Video Setting** page, accept the default settings by clicking **Next**

8 On the Capture Method page, click Next to transfer the entire tape at once

9 As your video transfers, you will see it playing in the preview page

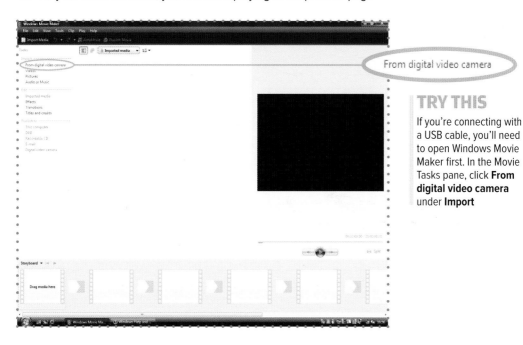

From digital video camera

TRY THIS

If you're connecting with a USB cable, you'll need to open Windows Movie Maker first. In the Movie Tasks pane, click **From digital video camera** under **Import**

BE CAREFUL

It's important to choose the right settings for a project as it can't be altered later. This can usually be done from the **Setup** menu. UK based camcorders are 'PAL' format; you may also need to check the camcorder documentation to be sure of format (MiniDV/HDV etc).

 # Videos

EDIT A VIDEO

Once you've saved your video clips onto your computer, you can edit them using video-editing software and create a new and improved piece of video. When editing, you can delete sections of video, move parts around, add special effects and transitions between clips, and more. You can also add a soundtrack or narrative to your video, and even create a DVD, complete with a menu, for easy navigation on your TV.

Tasks pane
Carry out tasks, such as importing videos or pictures from here.

Contents pane
Your imported video clips appear here.

Storyboard/Timeline
Drag your clips here to create your film.

Transitions
You can insert transitions (fade in or fade out, for example) between clips.

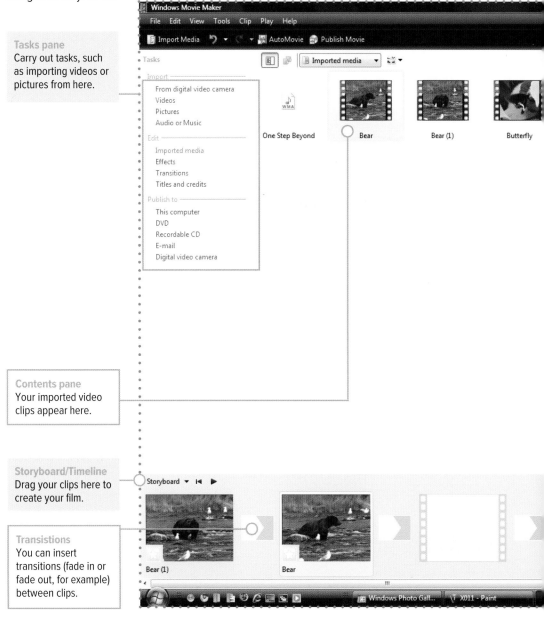

Basic video-editing software is often pre-installed on a new computer, or is supplied with your camera or camcorder. Windows Vista comes with Windows Movie Maker, for example. This offers most of the more common functions but, if you want something with more features, you can buy a more advanced software package.

Menu bar
The main toobar. From here you can save and edit your film, and access other options.

Preview screen
Preview your film in this window.

Storyboard: Bear

00:00:10.28 / 00:00:12.65

Split

23 July 2009,
Thursday

BE CAREFUL

Some camcorders can record in high-definition. If this is the case, you will need to make sure that your editing software is compatible with HD footage.

 **Videos**

Get started

Before you can start editing your video, you need to add the clips you want to use to the storyboard.

Storyboard view
This is the default view in Windows Movie Maker. It shows you the order of your clips and allows you to rearrange them. You can also see video effects and transitions that you've added.

1 Click

2 Click **All Programs**

3 Click **Windows Movie Maker**

4 To add a clip (that you've previously imported, see page 160), click **Import Media**

5 Click **Browse** and find the clip you want

6 Click **Import**

7 The clip will appear in the Contents pane.

8 This is the best time to put your clips in the order that you want them to be watched. Do this by dragging and dropping clips within the storyboard

9 You can drag a clip to the storyboard. Click on a clip in the Contents pane, keep the mouse button pressed down as you drag it to the storyboard. Let go at the location you want to drop it

TIP
You can increase the size of the preview pane by clicking and dragging the edge of the window.

TIP
You can click on the **Zoom** icon to magnify the timeline if you want to see it in more detail.

Jargon buster

Timeline view
This gives you a more detailed view of your project and allows you to make finer edits like adjusting the duration of transitions between clips.

Videos

Trim a clip

If some of your scenes are too long they can be trimmed before being edited into a whole.

1 If you're in Storyboard mode, switch to Timeline by clicking **View** on the menu bar. On the timeline, click the clip that you want to trim

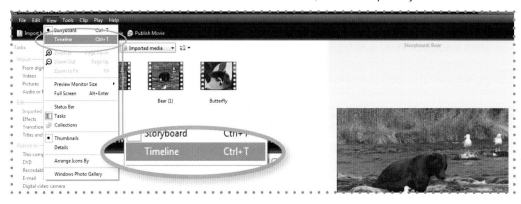

TIP

The trimmed part of a clip isn't deleted, it's just hidden so that it doesn't appear in your video.

2 Use the playback controls under the preview monitor to get to the point where you want the clip to begin. Click the **Pause** button

3 Click **Clip** then **Trim Beginning**

4 Repeat the process for the end of the clip – but this time click **Clip** and **Trim End**

Split a clip

If you want to add an effect between scenes – for example, you might
want to fade out and then fade in (see page 168) – you'll first need to split
your clip.

1 In the Contents pane or Timeline click the clip you want to split

2 Use the playback controls under the preview monitor to get to the
point where you want to split the clip

3 Click **Split**

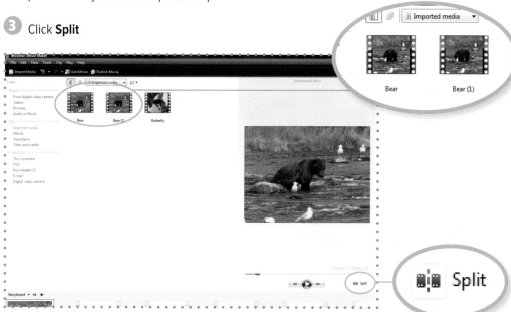

4 The two parts will now appear separately in the Contents pane

BE CAREFUL

With every major change
that you make, save a
copy of your project so
you don't lose it. (See
page 170 for how to do
this.)

TIP
You can also add a transition by dragging it to the timeline and dropping it into the desired slot.

Add transitions

A video can look a little clunky if the scenes are just sandwiched together. You can avoid this by adding transitions, such as a fade-in or fade-out effect.

1 On the Timeline, click on the clip that you want to appear after the transition

2 Click **Tools**

3 Click **Transitions**

4 In the Contents pane, click the transition you want to add from the selection available

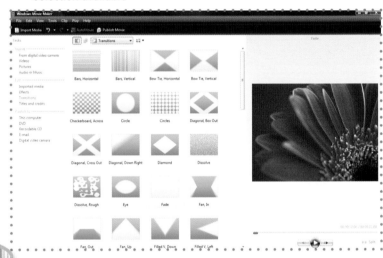

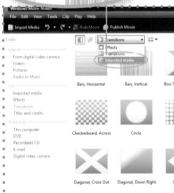

5 Click **Play** on the preview monitor to see a preview of what the transition will look like

6 Click **Clip** on the toolbar

7 Click **Add to Timeline**

8 To return to the Contents pane click the arrow next to Transitions and select Imported Media from the drop-down menu

Add music

You may want to add music to your video. Firstly, you'll need to add the music to your computer (see page 176 for how to do this), then you can use this in your newly created video.

1 Click **File**

2 Click **Import Media Items**

3 Find the file that you want to add and click on it (any audio is likely to be stored in your Music folder)

4 Click **Import**

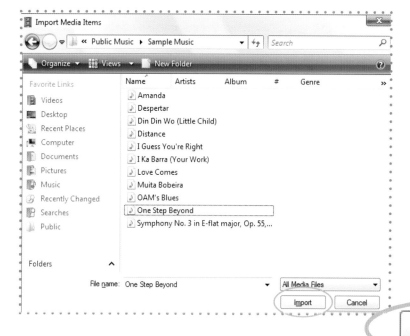

TRY THIS

At any point you can tweak the properties of an element of your project (clip, audio track, sound effects, transitions) by hovering the mouse cursor over it and right-clicking.

5 The music file will appear in the Contents pane. From here, drag it to the **Audio/Music** track of the timeline

TIP

To preview your video at any time, click on the **Play** button.

Videos

TIP

While you're editing your video it's known as a project.

Save an edited video

You should save your edited video regularly, so that you don't lose any of your changes should something go wrong.

1 Click **File**

2 If you haven't already given your project a name, click **Save Project As**, name it and then click **Save Project**. If it's already named, simply click **Save Project**

Publish and share a video

Saving your project just saves the settings and instructions on how you'd like your finished video to look. Once you're sure you're happy with it, to create a file that you can watch and share with others you will need to publish your clip.

1 Click **File**

2 Click **Publish Movie**

3 Click **This computer** and then **Next**

4 Type a name for your movie in the box that appears

5 In the **Publish to** box choose where you want to save your movie. Your Videos folder will be selected by default

6 Click **Next**

7 If you want to watch your movie once it's been published, select **Play movie when I click Finish**

8 Click **Publish** and wait while your movie is published. Depending on the length of your movie this could take a little while

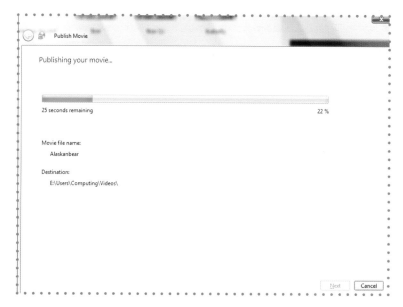

9 Click **Finish**

BE CAREFUL

Once you've published your movie you can't edit it. You can only edit the saved project so make sure you're happy with it first.

CREATE A DVD OF YOUR VIDEO

To burn a video to DVD, you need Windows DVD Maker. This is included with Vista Home Premium and Vista Ultimate. You also need a DVD burner – you may have one of these built into your computer, or you can buy a separate one to attach to your PC.

1 Insert a blank recordable or rewriteable DVD into your DVD burner (see page 8 for information)

2 Open **Windows Movie Maker** (see page 160)

3 Open the project you want to burn to DVD

4 Click **File**

5 Click **Publish Movie**

6 Click **DVD** and then **Next**

7 A window will pop up telling you that Windows DVD Maker is about to open. Click **OK**

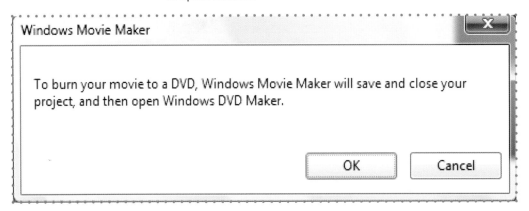

Windows Movie Maker

To burn your movie to a DVD, Windows Movie Maker will save and close your project, and then open Windows DVD Maker.

OK   Cancel

⑧ Click **Next**

⑨ Click **Burn**. This may take a little while

NEXT STEP ⊳

To find out how to
burn a CD of your
photos, see page 159.

Music

PLAY MUSIC

You can play a CD through your computer, in the same way as you would on your stereo.

TRY THIS

When you put a CD in, you may be asked how you want to play it. Click **Play using Windows Media Player**.

1 To play a CD, put in the CD drive and wait while the default music player on your computer starts up. This is likely to be Windows Media Player.

2 If it doesn't start up automatically click

3 Click **All Programs** and click on the CD in the list that appears.

Windows Media Player

Now Playing
Click on this and a slideshow of graphics will appear while you listen to music.

Library
The music you have stored on your computer will appear here.

Rip
Copy music from a CD on to your computer (see page 177).

Burn
Copy music on to a CD. To do this you'll need DVD burning software and a rewriteable disc drive (see page 8).

Jump between tracks with the Previous and Next buttons.

Volume
Alter the volume by dragging the dot.

Press play when a track is highlighted or double click on a particular track to listen to your CD.

DOWNLOAD MUSIC

As well as playing CDs and listening to music online, you can also download music from the internet. You can buy individual music tracks or even whole albums from sites such as iTunes, HMV and Tesco. For example, with HMV:

1. Go to www.hmv.co.uk

2. Click **Downloads**

3. Search for the song or album you want to buy by inputting keywords into the search box. Click on your choice

4. Click **Add to basket**

5. When you've finished shopping, click **Checkout**

TRY THIS

If you don't have speakers in your computer, you'll need to plug in headphones – look for the head-phones socket in your computer tower (it will have a headphones symbol).

music

TRY THIS

You can alter the volume by clicking on the Sound icon in the taskbar at the bottom of the screen.

6. HMV uses a Download Manager to download your music. This appears as a window showing the progress of your downloads

7. When it's finished, your music will appear in your Music folder. From here you can transfer it to an MP3 player (see page 179) or listen to it on your computer using software like Windows Media Player (see page 174)

NEXT STEP

For more on digital rights management, see page 182.

Music

CONVERT CDS TO MP3

TIP
By default your music will be saved to the Music folder.

Extracting the digital audio data from a CD and storing it on your PC is a process known as 'ripping'. You can build up a music library on your computer and then either transfer songs to an iPod or MP3 portable player or just listen to them on your PC.

Rip a CD using Windows Media Player

1 Click

2 Click **All Programs**

3 Click **Windows Media Player**

4 Insert a CD into the disc drive

5 Click **Rip** on the top toolbar

6 The title of the album should be displayed in the left-hand taskbar and the track listing should appear in the main part of the window

7 Click **Start Rip** to import the songs to your computer

Rip a CD using iTunes

1 Click

2 Click **All Programs**

3 Click **iTunes**

4 Insert a CD into the disc drive

5 The track listing for your album should appear in a window in the main library browser

6 Check under **Devices** in the left-hand taskbar – the album title should be listed next to an icon representing a compact disc

7 Click **Import CD**

Change the format of the file

By default, iTunes converts your CDs to AAC format. This is usually fine, but not all programs and devices are compatible with AAC, so you may want to switch to the more commonly used MP3 format.

1 In iTunes, click **Edit** on the toolbar

2 Click **Preferences** and then **General**

3 Click on **Import settings**

4 Under **Import Using**, select **MP3 Encoder**

5 Click **OK**

TIP
You can also open iTunes by clicking on the shortcut on your desktop.

USE AN MP3 PLAYER

MP3 players play music and films that you store digitally. These can either be copies of CDs you already own and have converted to digital files using your computer (see page 177), or music that you've downloaded to your computer from the internet (see page 175).

If you listen to your music on an Apple iPod, you probably use iTunes to manage your music. iTunes is much like Windows Media Player, but includes the ability to download music.

Select your music

1 Open **iTunes** on your computer

2 Connect your music player to your computer. To do this, you'll need to use the lead that came with your player. Connect one end to the correctly shaped socket on your player and connect the other end to you computer's USB socket (see page 12)

3 Wait a few moments. The name of your music player will appear in the list on the left-hand side of the screen under the heading **Devices**

4 The first time you connect your music player to your computer, you'll see a message asking if you want to sync songs automatically. If you say yes, whenever you connect your music player to your computer, any new music that's stored in your iTunes library will automatically be added to your player, and any music that you've removed from iTunes will be removed from your player. This is the easiest option

5 It's not always possible to sync everything automatically, though. For example, you might have so many songs in your iTunes library that they won't all fit on your player. If this is the case, you can select individual playlists to add instead (see page 181 for creating a playlist)

6 With your music player selected in the left-hand panel, click on the **Music tab**. Select **Sync music** followed by **Selected playlists**

7 Tick the boxes next to the playlists you want to add, tick if you have any music videos you want to add to your player, and tick if you'd like your player to display the album cover of each of your tracks. When you're ready, click **Sync**

8 You can also select individual tracks to add. On the **Summary** tab choose the option **Manually manage music and video** and click **Apply**

Transfer music to an MP3 player

1 To add songs to your music player, select **Music** from the list on the left-hand side of the iTunes screen. This brings up the list of all the songs in your iTunes library.

2 Select a track by clicking on it and holding down the left-hand mouse button, then dragging it over to where your music player is listed (under **Devices**). Let go of the mouse button and that track will have been copied onto your music player. You can do the same thing with playlists – click on a playlist, drag it over to where your music player is listed and drop it in

3 If you're managing your music manually as opposed to syncing automatically, you'll need to eject your iPod from iTunes before disconnecting. Click on the little upwards facing arrow beside your iPod's name on the iTunes screen and wait for your iPod to say that it's OK to disconnect

Music

CREATE A PLAYLIST

A playlist allows you to group together songs like a compilation. It might be for when you're in a certain mood, and allows you to move all those songs together (see page 180).

(see page 180)

Using Windows Media Player

1 Click

2 Click **All Programs**

Chilled out

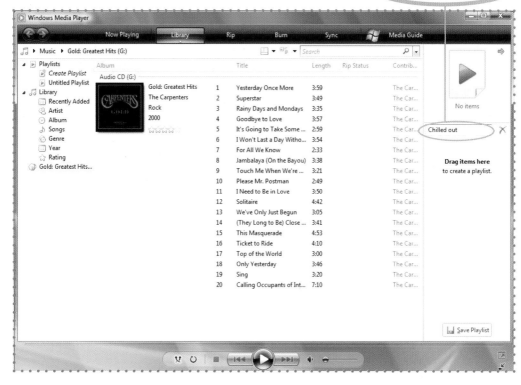

3 Click **Windows Media Player**

4 Click **Library**

5 Click **Create Playlist**

6 Type in a name for your playlist, for example, Chilled Out

⑦ Add songs by dragging and dropping (see page 12) tracks onto the area below your playlist title (if you can't see your music, click on **Library**)

⑧ When you've finished, click **Save Playlist**

Using iTunes

You can create a playlist manually using iTunes or you can let iTunes create one for you based on specific criteria.

① Click

② Click **All Programs**

③ Click **iTunes**. Click **File** on the top toolbar

④ Click **New Smart Playlist**

⑤ A small dialogue box will open and allow you automatically to add songs that match a set of special 'rules'

⑥ Choose a rule by selecting criteria from the drop-down menus. For example, as on the screenshot below, select **Genre** from the first list, then **Contains** from the second, then type **Classical** into the box and click the plus ('+') button on the right to create a classical playlist

⑦ You can add more rules and further refine your playlist by putting a tick next to **Limit to** and setting the size or duration options

⑧ Click **OK** and type in a name for your playlist

Digital rights management

One of the most contentious issues for downloaders of music is digital rights management (DRM). This is an anti-piracy technique that enables companies to retain some control over what you can and can't do with the file you've downloaded, such as how many times you can copy it either to a CD or to another machine.

However, it's becoming increasingly easy to find tracks that don't have DRM restrictions. Many music websites now offer MP3 downloads without DRM, and these tracks can be played on all MP3 players, including iPods. Sony BMG is the last of the 'big four' record companies to abandon DRM, having agreed to follow the lead of EMI, Universal and Warner.

TRY THIS

You can also download 'podcasts' – radio programmes and TV clips – to listen to on your MP3 player or computer. Many of these are free. Take a look at www.apple. com/podcasting to get started.

BE CAREFUL

For tips on shopping safely online see page 102.

NEXT STEP ▶

Find out how to transfer music from you computer onto your MP3 player on page 180.

MAINTAIN YOUR PC

By reading and following all the steps in this chapter, you will get to grips with:

- **Backing up important files**

- **Cleaning up your desktop**

- **Uninstalling programs**

BACK UP DATA

It is important to make copies of your important photographs and documents so that, should something like a hard disk failure or virus happen to your computer, you don't lose them. You can back up data by saving it to a memory stick, external hard drive – both of which should be stored separately to the PC – or using an online backup service, which saves your data for you online.

Jargon buster

Memory stick
A small device that plugs into your computer and can be used to save files on to. Also known as a USB key or flash drive.

SAVE FILES ON A MEMORY STICK

1 Plug your memory stick into the USB port of your computer

2 Your computer should recognise that you've plugged in an external device. An icon and popup message will appear in the taskbar at the bottom of your screen

3 Open the file you want to save to your memory stick. Click **File**, then **Save As**

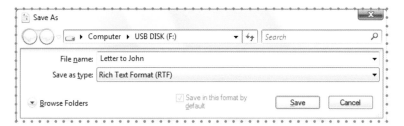

4 Click on your memory stick in the left-hand side of the window. This will often be referred to as Removable Disk or USB disk; it will also be assigned a letter. Click **Save**

5 To remove the memory stick, right click on its icon in the taskbar and click **Safely remove USB Mass Storage Device** (the wording may vary depending on the type of memory stick you're using)

6 Remove the memory stick

7 To access your files in the future, just plug in the memory stick, click on the icon on the taskbar and a window will appear from where you can open your files

USE AN EXTERNAL HARD DRIVE

An external hard drive is an easy way of adding additional storage to your PC. You can also use it for backing up vital data in case your main hard drive has problems, or to provide more space if your PC's hard drive is filling up. They will connect directly to a USB port on your PC, which is much simpler than installing an additional hard drive inside your PC.

The two main types of external hard drive are desktop and portable. Desktop drives are larger and heavier, and require a separate power supply – well suited to being a permanent companion to your desktop. Portable drives are smaller and lighter, and draw their power from the PC – ideal for transferring files between PCs.

Set up an external hard drive

1 Connect your external hard drive to your computer using the USB cable provided with it

2 The new drive should already be set up and a window will appear

3 Click **Open folder to view files** and then close the folder window by clicking on the cross

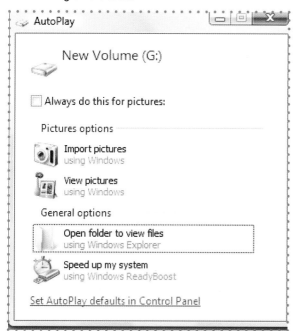

Jargon buster

External Hard Drive
A storage device that plugs into your PC. Useful for saving copies of important files or creatiing additional storage.

185

4 If Windows doesn't automatically recognise the drive, click and right click on **Computer**

5 Select **Manage**, then **Disk Management**

6 Your new disk will appear in the list (usually as Disk 1 or Disk 2). Right click on it and select **New Simple Volume**

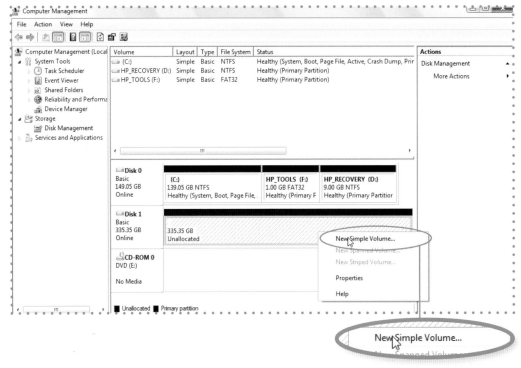

TRY THIS

Windows Home Basic doesn't allow you to set up automatic backups. In this case, if you want to set a backup schedule, you need to buy separate backup software.

Once you've set up your external hard drive you can save files on to it manually (this is a similar process to saving to a memory stick, page 184).

Alternatively you can set up a backup schedule to save copies of your important files automatically. You can do this using Vista's Backup and Restore Center, see opposite. Bear in mind that this requires your external hard drive to be plugged in continually, so isn't ideal if you're concerned about theft. If you have important files on your hard drive, it may be preferable to store your external hard drive away from your computer.

BACK UP FILES

You can use Vista's Backup and Restore Center to back up your important files and set up automatic backups.

1 Click ![] and then click **Control Panel**

2 Click **System and Maintenance**

3 Click **Backup and Restore Center**

4 Click **Back up files**. A window will appear asking where you want to save your files

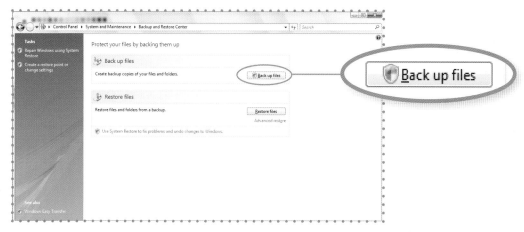

5 Click the arrow. Select from the drop-down menu where to save your backup. Click **Next**

6 Now choose which file types you want to back up – for example, picture or music files. Click **Next**

7 Choose how often you want your computer to create a backup. The drop-down menus will reveal more options

8 Click **Save settings and start backup**

Restore files

Should you need to restore files (for example, if you lose a file, it becomes corrupt or is changed accidentally), go to the Backup and Restore Center and click **Restore files**.

FULL-SYSTEM BACKUP

As well as backing up your files, you can back up your entire computer (including the operating system – see page 8 – and all programs). This is useful if your computer is affected by a virus and you need to restore everything.

In Vista, only Vista Ultimate allows you to create a full system backup; if you're using other versions of Vista, you will need to invest in separate backup software to do this. Alternatively, Vista's System Restore tool (page 212) may be able to help you if something goes wrong.

BACKUP TIPS

What data do I need to back up?

You need to make frequent backup copies of any personal files – photos, videos, music, emails, documents, spreadsheets and the like – but you should also consider making a 'full' backup of your PC's system files and installed applications every so often too.

How often should I back up my computer?

When you set your backup schedule, you'll first have to tell the backup software exactly what you want to safeguard. You'll probably be asked to choose the type of file (music, images, word processing, etc.) you want to back up, or specific folders. You can then schedule your backup frequency. This will depend on the type of data you're protecting – if it's key work documents that change every day, then it's probably worth backing up daily, but if it's a collection of digital photos that only get added to every few weeks, then a weekly backup is sufficient.

What's the difference between incremental and full system backups?

An incremental backup checks to see which files and folders have been altered since the last time you backed up, and updates your backup copies as necessary. A full system backup makes a 'clone' or disk image of your entire hard drive and enables you to restore your whole system from scratch. The downside is that the resulting file can be enormous, so you'll need an external hard drive (see page 185) and backup software.

Do I need special software to back up?

You can use Vista's Backup and Restore Center to make copies of important files, but only the Ultimate edition of Vista comes with software to create a full system backup. You'll need to buy a dedicated backup software package if you don't have Vista Ultimate, along with an external hard drive on which to store the system backup.

Can I back up my data online?

There are several services that offer online backup, including Carbonite (www.carbonite.com, costing approximately £25 per year).

Can I back up to DVD?

Blank DVDs are a good way of backing up medium-sized amounts of data (around 4GB per disc). But, as they're prone to getting scratched, they're not as reliable as memory sticks, which can hold more data.

Spring-clean your PC

DELETE A FILE

Over time, your computer becomes full of old information, such as Word documents and spreadsheets. If you no longer use these, it is worth deleting them to increase the available space for new files you want to create.

1 Hold down the Windows key (see page 13) on your keyboard and press E to launch Windows Explorer – the application that helps you search for files

2 Navigate to the folder where the file is stored

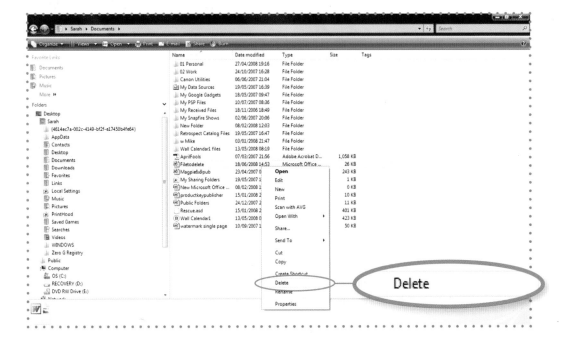

3 Left click once on the file icon to select it

4 Then right click and select **Delete** from the list

5 A separate dialogue box will pop up and ask you if you're sure you want to delete the file. Click **Yes**. Your file will now disappear from the folder

USE THE RECYCLE BIN

When you delete a file, it's held in the Recycle Bin. Files in the Recycle Bin take up valuable space on your hard drive so you should clear it out occasionally.

Delete a file from the Recycle Bin

1 Right click on the **Recycle Bin** icon on your desktop

2 Click on **Empty Recycle Bin** in the drop-down menu

3 A window will appear asking if you're sure you want to continue. Click **Yes**

BE CAREFUL
Before emptying the Recycle Bin, make sure there's nothing in there that you want.

Delete Multiple Items

Are you sure you want to permanently delete these 9 items?

Yes   No

Retrieve a file from the Recycle Bin

If you accidentally delete a file, you can still retrieve it from the Recycle Bin (as long as you haven't emptied the bin in between).

1 Double click on the **Recycle Bin** icon on your desktop. You'll see a list of your deleted files

2 Right click on the file you want to recover and click **Restore**. The file will reappear in its original location

Spring-clean your PC

FREE UP SPACE ON YOUR HARD DRIVE

When you're using your computer frequently it can quickly become clogged up with information that can slow it down. You can free up space on your computer's hard drive by using a program called Disk Cleanup, which will remove any temporary files and unnecessary system files, as well as emptying your Recycle Bin.

1 Click then **All Programs**

2 Click **Accessories**

3 Click **System Tools**

4 Click **Disk Cleanup**

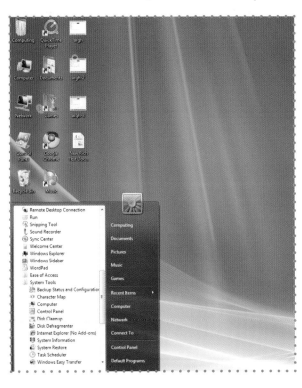

5 In the **Disk Cleanup Options** box that opens, choose whether you want to clean up all the files on your computer, or just your personal documents

6 Select the hard disk you want to clean up. For most people, this will show up as the C: drive. Click **OK**

7 A window will appear while the Disk Cleanup tool calculates how much space it will be able to free up

8 Select the files you want to delete by ticking the boxes. Click on an entry to see a description at the bottom of the window if you're unsure what the files relate to

9 Click **OK**

CLEAN OUT YOUR WEB BROWSER

When you surf the internet, files (known as a cache) are saved onto your computer. These hold details about the site you've visited (known as stored cookies). This can be handy and can save you time. For example, when you log into your eBay account, you can tick a box so that it remembers your details and logs you in automatically whenever you go to the home page.

However, by cleaning out your internet cache and deleting stored cookies, you can clear some space on your hard disk, and possibly speed up your broadband connection speed. This will also protect your privacy if other people are using your computer as they will be unable to see what you've been looking at.

1 In Internet Explorer, click **Tools**

2 Click **Internet Options**

3 Click the **General** tab

4 Under **Browsing history**, click **Delete**

5 To clear your cache click **Delete files**. Click **Yes**

6 Also click **Delete cookies**. Click **Yes**

7 Click **Close**

8 Click **OK**

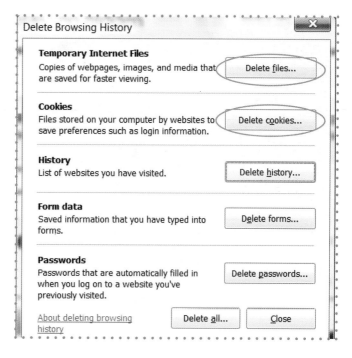

Delete Browsing History

Temporary Internet Files
Copies of webpages, images, and media that are saved for faster viewing.
Delete files...

Cookies
Files stored on your computer by websites to save preferences such as login information.
Delete cookies...

History
List of websites you have visited.
Delete history...

Form data
Saved information that you have typed into forms.
Delete forms...

Passwords
Passwords that are automatically filled in when you log on to a website you've previously visited.
Delete passwords...

About deleting browsing history
Delete all...   Close

UPDATE WINDOWS

Windows is constantly being updated, with additions to its software that can both prevent and fix known problems. You can check to make sure that your computer has all the latest updates and install any new updates.

1 Click ⊕ then **All Programs**

2 Click **Windows Update**

3 Click **Check for updates**

4 Windows will search for any updates your computer needs

5 If any updates are found, a box will tell you. Click **Install updates**

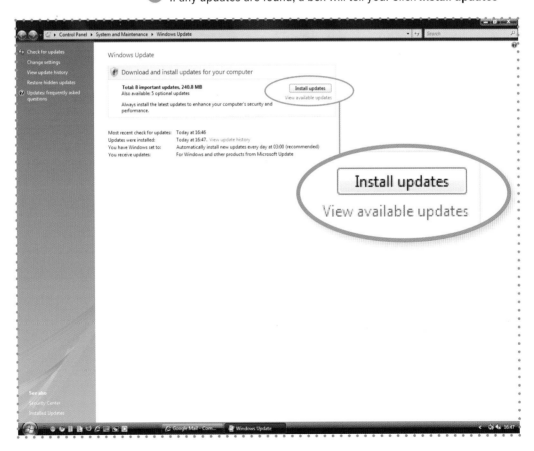

Install updates automatically

1 Click [image] then **All Programs**

2 Click **Windows Updates**

3 Click **Change settings**

4 Make sure that the box titled **Install updates automatically (recommended)** is checked

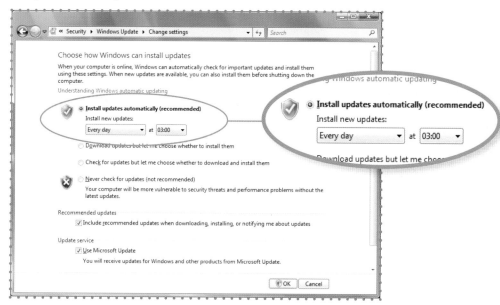

5 Click the downward pointing arrows to select how regularly to install updates (daily is recommended) and choose a time of day

6 Under **Recommended updates**, select **Include recommended updates when downloading, installing, or notifying me about updates**

7 Click **OK**

TRY THIS

You can also install optional updates – for example, updating your web browser. Go to windowsupdate.microsoft.com for more info (you don't need to type www as with usual websites).

Spring-clean your PC

UNINSTALL UNUSED PROGRAMS

Removing unused programs will free up valuable space on your hard drive. For example, you might have installed a Sudoku game or some video-editing software that you no longer use.

1 If the program you want to uninstall is open, first close it down

2 Click then **Control Panel**

3 Click **Programs**

4 Click **Programs and Features**

5 Click **Uninstall a program**

6 Click on the program you would like to remove, then click **Uninstall**

TIP

To uninstall a program you may need to reinsert the disc you used to install it, so keep any discs safe.

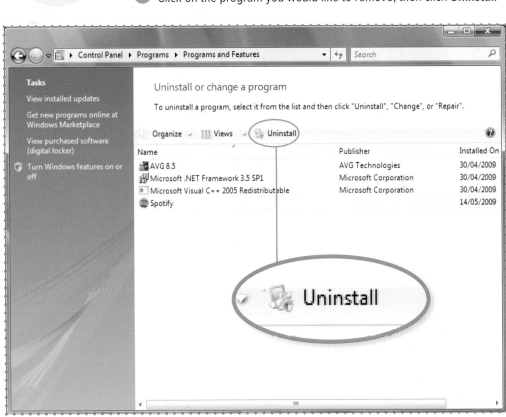

SECURITY

By reading and following all the steps in this chapter, you will get to grips with:

- **Security threats to watch out for**

- **Scanning your PC for viruses and spyware**

- **Protecting yourself online**

TYPES OF SECURITY THREAT

There are numerous security threats out there that could potentially damage your computer or jeopardise your personal information. With the proper precautions there's no need to worry, though – see opposite.

DoS attacks
What is it?
DoS, or 'Denial of Service', attacks aim to disrupt the online services of companies and organisations.

Potential risk
Home users are unlikely to be the intended target. More at risk are government agencies, banks and other important institutions, whose network, website or communications could be disrupted by a DoS attack.

Phishing
What is it?
An email that appears to be from an official source but is actually a sophisticated fake, designed to get you to part with personal information.

Potential risk
Phishing emails are convincing. They look like they come from an official body (see page 137). Clicking on links and entering passwords or financial details could mean that you hand over the keys to your bank account.

Spam
What is it?
Spam is unsolicited junk email, often purporting to sell you things like medication and sent out in bulk by automated web robots (see page 132).

Potential risk
Spam can clog up networks and make sending and receiving email annoying. Many phishing emails are spam.

Spyware
What is it?
Software that installs itself on your computer without your knowledge.

Potential risk
Once installed, spyware can get in the way of the ordinary operation of your computer. Spyware can cause your computer to flash up warnings

and messages, change your computer settings or cripple its functions. Worse still, some spyware is capable of literally spying on your activities and collecting personal information (see page 202).

Trojan
What is it?
A program that gets through your computer's defences disguised as something else – like the Trojan Horse.

Potential risk
Running the disguised program could install dangerous software on your PC, allowing hackers to access or delete your data via the internet.

Worm
What is it?
A computer program designed to make copies of itself, which it sends to other computers.

Potential risk
As well as slowing down networks, worms can sometimes contain software that might damage your PC or open a back door to hackers.

SECURE YOUR PC
To protect your computer and the data on it from attack, you need to have several different types of security software installed on your PC – and keep them all up to date. To protect your computer fully you need to install:

A firewall This is a piece of software that sits between your PC and the internet, protecting your computer from incoming attacks from hackers or malware such as viruses. It's vital that your firewall is switched on (see page 201).

Anti-virus software This protects against a number of different types of threat, including Trojans and worms. Some anti-virus software will include anti-spyware tools too (see page 202).

Anti-spyware software This protects your computer from spyware (malicious software that downloads to your computer without your knowledge). Spyware can monitor your activity and collect information about you (see page 203 for more on scanning for spyware).

TIP
The Windows Vista operating system features both firewall and anti-spyware software.

TIP

You may be offered discounted or free security software when you buy a new computer.

Jargon buster

Trojan
A computer virus that disguises itself as an innocent program to entice people to install it. Trojans can allow third parties complete access to your computer remotely.

Jargon buster

Worm
Similar to a virus, except a worm doesn't need to attach itself to a document and can simply spread via the internet.

Security software
You can buy a security suite that contains all the elements that you'll need. It may also contain additional features such as a backup program to help you to copy important files, or parental control software so that you can manage your child's internet use.

Once installed, security software runs automatically when your PC is on. It scans every file on your machine to spot existing viruses and can take upwards of two hours.

To ensure that you're properly protected:

▶ Download regular security updates. Your chosen program should be set to do this automatically

▶ If you want to use the version built into your suite, you'll need to switch off the Windows Vista firewall as you can't run more than one of these at a time

▶ Don't install more than one suite at once as two anti-virus programs or two firewalls can conflict. The exception to this rule is anti-spyware where you can use several programs, though only one of these should be set for automatic scanning

▶ Security suites can place high demands on your computer's system resources. If your PC only just meets the requirements of a suite, it's worth looking for an alternative

Free software
Rather than buying a suite, you can download free security programs online. For example, AVG offer a free version of their anti-virus software (free.avg.com).

The downside of free programs is that you'll have to download individual programs from different places and you won't get the integrated approach that you'll experience with a bundled suite. You'll have to maintain and monitor each aspect separately (for instance, ensuring that the updates are working) and you're unlikely to get the kind of support you'd receive with a paid-for suite. If you have problems you may need to search the manufacturer's support pages for assistance.

TURN ON THE FIREWALL

A firewall protects your computer from incoming attacks from hackers or malware such as viruses, so it's vital that your firewall is switched on. To turn on the Vista firewall:

1 Click then **Control panel**

2 Click **Security** and click on **Windows firewall**

TIP

For more on how to stay safe online, see page 205.

3 You should see a green shield icon if the firewall is switched on. If not, click **Turn Windows firewall on or off** in the sidebar

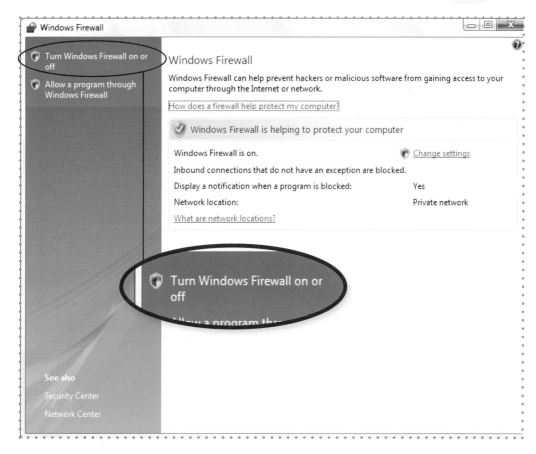

4 Click **Continue** and tick the box to turn on the firewall

ANTI-VIRUS SOFTWARE EXPLAINED

The best security programs can be set to run largely by themselves, but there are a few things you should know about maintaining your anti-virus software. Here are answers to some of the most common questions.

Does Windows have anti-virus software?
No – neither Vista nor XP come with anti-virus protection. You'll need to use a third-party product.

How do I know my anti-virus software is on?
Most anti-virus programs put an icon in the Taskbar (bottom right) to show that they're switched on. You can also check by going to Windows Security Center (see page 20 for more information on this).

How can I tell if my computer has a virus?
If your computer becomes slow or unresponsive, or if you find that programs you use all the time are behaving in an unusual way, then your computer may have been infected by a virus.

How many anti-virus programs should I run?
You need to run only one anti-virus program. You should also run a firewall and an anti-spyware program.

What's the difference between anti-spyware and anti-virus software?
Anti-virus software protects you against viruses that arrive via email messages or infected files. Anti-spyware programs check for and eliminate other types of malicious software that hide within a program you have chosen to install.

How do I scan for viruses?
Generally, the **Scan** option should be accessible from the main program page of your anti-virus software. Check your anti-virus program's settings for a scheduling option that lets you run a weekly automated scan.

How often should I update my anti-virus software?
Update your anti-virus program daily. The best anti-virus programs can be set to look for and retrieve updates automatically. In other cases, you may see a message pop up to alert you when updates are available.

SCAN FOR SPYWARE

If your computer becomes slow or is acting strangely, it could be due to spyware. You can check for spyware using anti-spyware programs such as Microsoft Defender (included with Windows Vista).

1 Open **Windows Defender** by clicking then **Control Panel**

2 Click **Security**

3 Click on **Windows Defender**

4 Click **Scan** to scan your computer for spyware. The scan may take a few minutes. You can then choose to ignore, remove or quarantine files

TIP

To find out what else you need to do to protect your PC, see page 204.

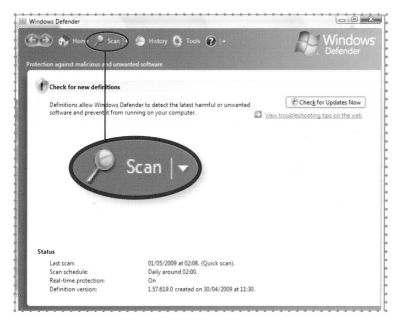

5 To set your computer to run an automatic, daily scan, click **Tools** then **Options**

6 Using the drop-down arrows, select a daily scan and your preferred time for the scan to run. Using the drop-down menus, you can also tell Defender what to do when it finds, for instance, high alert items

7 Click **Save** and **Continue**

PC SECURITY TIPS

Keep your security software up to date

Security software is only as good as its last update. With new virus and spyware threats constantly emerging, software manufacturers issue regular security updates in response to reported threats. Update your security software at least once a week. Many programs allow you to set it up so that it updates automatically – you can usually find this option under the Settings menu.

Take care when downloading

When you're downloading free security software, check the name of the product carefully, as some names sound like familiar sources, but are not. Make sure you've downloaded the software from a trusted source.

To ensure that you download the right program, type in the full address of the security software's website in the address bar of your browser rather than typing the program's name into a search engine.

Steer clear of websites or programs asking for money.

Create strong passwords

Protect yourself by not storing passwords or login details on your computer.

Don't use a single password for every account you use online.

A strong password consists of a mixture of letters (upper and lower case) and numbers.

NEXT STEP ▶

For more on backing up your data, see page 184 onwards.

Back up your data

It's crucial to back up your important files regularly. Should something happen to your computer, you could lose all of your data. You need to make frequent backup copies of any personal files – photos, videos, emails, for example – but you should also consider making a 'full' backup of your PC's system files and installed applications every so often too.

INTERNET SECURITY TIPS

Delete your browser history

Your web browser stores a list of the websites you've visited. This means that anyone who uses your computer can view a list of all the websites that you've been to. To delete your Internet Explorer browser history:

1 In Internet Explorer, click **Tools**

2 Click **Internet options**

3 Select the **General** tab

4 Under **Browsing history**, select **Delete**

5 Click **Delete history** in the new window that appears

6 Click **Close**. Then click **Yes**

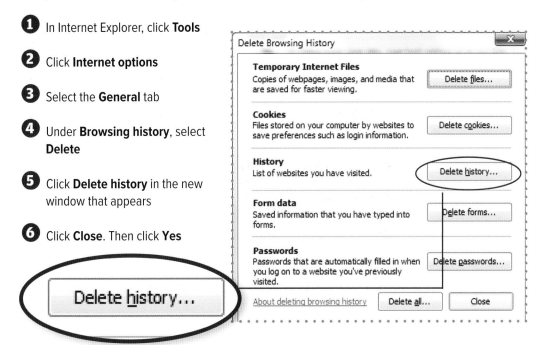

Turn off autocomplete

Autocomplete is a function that allows some browsers to 'remember' what you put into online forms. This is useful if you frequently log in to the same sites or are often required to fill in your details in online forms. However, it also means that anyone with access to your computer can see all these details at the click of a button. For shared computers you may wish to turn this off.

1 In Internet Explorer, click **Tools**

2 Click **Internet options**

3 Select the **Content** tab

Security

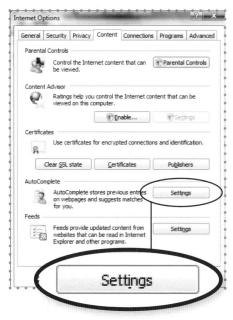

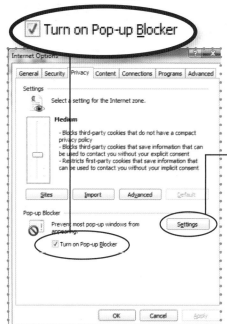

4 Under **Autocomplete** click **Settings**

5 Remove the ticks next to **Forms** and **Usernames and passwords on forms**

6 Click **OK**, then **OK** again

Block pop-ups

Pop-ups are small windows that open automatically when you visit certain web pages. Many are just annoying or confusing, but they can also contain malicious code or phishing scams. To block pop-ups in Internet Explorer:

1 In Internet Explorer, click **Tools**

2 Click **Internet options**

3 Select the **Privacy** tab, and make sure that there's a tick next to **Turn on pop-up blocker**

4 If you want to allow pop-ups, but only from trusted websites, click on **Settings** and enter your selected web addresses

Secure web pages

Be alert when you're asked to enter personal details such as your credit card details into a web page. A secure web page is prefixed 'https' (the extra 's' stands for secure). You should also check for a padlock icon in your address bar, which denotes a secure web page.

TROUBLE SHOOTING

By reading and following all the steps in this chapter, you will get to grips with:

▶ **Checking your computer's specifications**

▶ **Using Windows Help tools**

▶ **Restoring your PC**

Troubleshooting

CHECK THE COMPUTER'S SPECIFICATIONS

Before you can find out what's wrong with it, you may need more information about it. To find out your computer's specifications – for example, the type of processor it has and how much memory is installed – follow these steps:

1 Click ⊞ then **Control Panel**

2 Click **System and Maintenance**

3 Click **System.** This brings up a box showing basic information about your computer

4 To get further information on your graphics card, sound card, etc., click **Device Manager** from the left-hand menu

5 You'll see a list of different types of hardware. Right click on a device you'd like to know more about

TIP

To find out more about the parts of your computer, see pages 8–9.

> Control Panel ▸ System | Search
>
> **Tasks**
> Device Manager
> Remote settings
> System protection
> Advanced system settings
>
> View basic information about your computer
>
> Windows edition
>
> Windows Vista™ Home Premium
> Copyright © 2007 Microsoft Corporation. All rights reserved.
> Service Pack 2
> Upgrade Windows Vista
>
> System
> Rating: 3.0 Windows Experience Index : Unrated
> Processor: Intel(R) Xeon(TM) CPU 3.20GHz   3.19 GHz
> Memory (RAM):   2.00 GB
> System type: 32-bit Operating System
>
> Computer name, domain, and workgroup settings
> Computer name: Computing-PC   Change settings
> Full computer name: Computing-PC
> Computer description:
> Workgroup: WORKGROUP
>
> Windows activation
>
> **See also**
> Windows Update
> Security Center
> Performance

6 Select **Properties** to see more details

USE WINDOWS HELP

Windows Vista comes with a selection of built-in tools that can help you identify and put right many common computer problems. To access Windows Help:

1 Click 🪟 then **Help and Support**

2 The **Help** console will open

3 To search for a particular subject, type some keywords into the search box (for example, Windows Mail or desktop icons)

4 Press **Enter** and click on the relevant search result

Further help

Microsoft also has an online support database called the Knowledge Base. This can be useful, since it's updated all the time and may have more recent information relating to your problem. You can broaden your search by setting the Help console to include results from the Knowledge Base. You'll need to be connected to the internet for this to work:

1 Click **Options** on the toolbar

2 Click **Settings**

3 In the box that appears put a tick next to **Include Windows Online Help and Support when you search for help**. Up-to-date online results will now be included in any future searches you carry out

troubleshooting

▶ Troubleshooting

GET HELP ONLINE

If you know that your problem lies with a specific program, such as Windows, or a device, such as your DVD drive, then your first port of call should be the website of that manufacturer. Once you're on the site, have a look for a link that says **Support** or **Help**. Click it and check out the frequently asked questions (FAQs) section, where you'll find common problems and solutions.

On some websites, you can also post a message in an online forum asking for help, send the support team an email or have a one-to-one online chat with a technician.

Error messages

Error messages are a useful way to track down a solution to a specific problem. If your computer is throwing up an error message, make a precise note of what it says or use your cursor to highlight the message and press **Ctrl + C** to copy it. Next, enter the error message into a search engine such as www.google.co.uk or www.yahoo.co.uk (type it in, or press **Ctrl + V** to paste it straight in), and press **Search**.

If you can't find anything useful in the results that come up, have a go at typing a brief description of your problem and then running a new search. And, if at first you don't succeed, reword your problem and try again.

Using forums

If you can't find a solution with a general internet search, try searching the list of useful websites and forums opposite.

If the sites listed don't provide the answer to your specific problem you can post your question in one of the forums. Include the full details of your problem, including error messages and any relevant make and model information, and state which operating system (Windows Vista or XP, for example) you're using. Bear in mind, though, that the respondents aren't necessarily qualified computer experts.

Useful websites and forums

www.annoyances.org
Collection of advice that's great for solving Windows-related problems

www.askdavetaylor.com
Expert advice on a wide variety of technical topics

www.bleepingcomputer.com
Online community that has tutorials, forums and tips

www.compukiss.com
'Keeping It Short and Simple', this site is great for tips

www.computerhope.com
A support site with good forums

www.computing.net
Offers useful, active forums

www.geekstogo.com
Forums that allow you to take advantage of helpful technicians

www.supportfreaks.com
Use the 'Freebies' service to get support

http://support.microsoft.com
Microsoft's official support site for those using Windows PCs

www.which.co.uk
Lots of computing and security help and advice.
To contact the Which? Computing Helpdesk service, go to
www.which.co.uk/computinghelpdesk. You'll need to have the
code CME50BOOK0909 to hand and input it where it asks for
your membership number. See page 224 for more information.

▶ Troubleshooting

RESTORE YOUR PC

If you're unable to fix your computer yourself, you can use a feature called System Restore. It works by taking a snapshot of your system settings and then, if something goes wrong, it's possible to roll back your PC and restore it to one of these points.

Set a restore point

1 Click ⊞ then **Control Panel**

2 Click **System and Maintenance**, then **Backup and Restore Center**

3 Click on **Use System Restore to fix problems and undo changes to Windows**

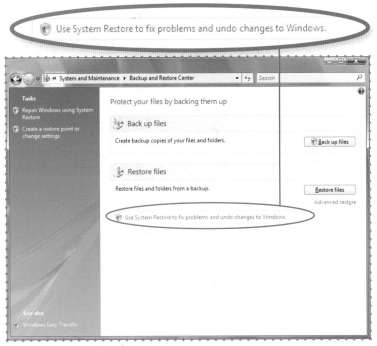

4 Click **Open System Protection**, click **Create**

5 Name your restore point and click **Create**

6 Click **OK**, then **OK** again

Restore your computer

1 Open **System Restore** as in steps 1 to 3 above

2 Click **Next**

3 Select the restore point to which you want your computer to return

4 Click **Next**, then **Finish**

▌BE CAREFUL

System Restore is no replacement for proper backup; it won't save copies of your personal files and can't remove virus infections. See page 184 onwards for more on proper backing up.

JARGON BUSTER

3G The third generation of mobile networks, which allows large amounts of data to be sent wirelessly. Mobile broadband operates over the 3G network.

ADSL (Asymmetric digital subscriber line) A way of sending data over a copper wire telephone line.

Adware Software that tracks your web use to determine your interests and deliver relevant adverts.

Anti-spyware Software that prevents and/or removes spyware.

Anti-virus Software that scans for viruses and removes them from your computer.

Application A type of program that's used by a person, as opposed to a program that's used by a computer.

Backup A copy of your files or programs for safekeeping.

Blog A regularly updated online journal.

Broadband A method of connecting to the internet via cable or ADSL (see above). Much faster than a dial-up connection.

Browser The software that enables you to view web pages. Often these contain phishing filters.

Cursor A cursor is the symbol on the screen that shows where the next character will appear.

Desktop The main screen you see when you start your computer. From here you can organise and access programs.

Dial-up An internet connection via a normal phone line, which is slow compared to broadband.

Dongle A small device that connects to a computer's USB port. In this context, it enables you to connect to the internet.

Download To transfer data from a remote computer to your own computer over the internet.

Driver Software that allows your computer to communicate with other devices, such as a printer.

Email client A computer program that manages emails. Emails are stored on your computer, and you only need to be connected to the internet to send and receive emails.

Ethernet A means of connecting computers together using cables – a common method for networking computers.

External hard drive A storage device that plugs into your PC. Useful for saving copies of important files, or creating additional storage.

File extension The letters that appear after a file name. They show what type of document it is.

Firewall Software (or hardware) that blocks unwanted communication from, and often to, the internet.

FireWire A type of connection that is fast and well-suited to transferring large amounts of data, such as video footage, from devices. FireWire cables plug directly into a FireWire port on your computer.

Flash drive See **Memory stick**

Forum An online message board.

Gigabytes (GB) A measurement of data storage. Eight bits make up a byte; 1,024 bytes make a kilobyte; 1,024 kilobytes make a megabyte; 1,024 megabytes make a gigabyte.

Hard disk The main long-term storage space used by your computer to store data. Also known as a hard drive.

Hard drive See **Hard disk**

Icon A small picture that represents an object or program.

Instant messaging A form of communication allowing two or more people to hold a conversation in real time by typed messages over the internet.

ISP (internet service provider) An ISP is the company that enables and services your connection to the internet.

Malware Malicious software. A generic term for any program that is harmful to your computer, for example, a virus.

Mbps (Megabits per second) A measure of the speed of data transfer, often used when talking about the speed of broadband.

Megabyte (Mb) A measurement of data storage. Eight bits make up a byte; 1,024 bytes make a kilobyte; 1,024 kilobytes make a megabyte; 1,024 megabytes make a gigabyte.

Megahertz (MHz) The speed of your computer's processor (its brain) is measured in megahertz. One MHz represents one million cycles per second.

Memory stick Small, portable device used to store and transfer data. It plugs into a USB port and is also called a USB key, flash drive or pen drive.

Microfilter A device that attaches to your telephone socket and enables you to make voice calls and use broadband at the same time via ADSL.

Modem A device that allows a computer to send information over a telephone line. You need a modem to connect to the internet.

MP3 player A portable music player that plays digital music.

Network A system of communication between two or more computers.

Operating System The software that manages your computer.

PDF A file that captures all the graphics, fonts and formatting of a document, regardless of the application in which it was created.

Pen drive See **Memory stick**

Phishing A type of email scam where you're tricked into giving away personal details by being directed to a spoof website that resembles the site of an official organisation (a bank, for example).

Podcast A type of online radio (or video) show that you can subscribe to. Files are downloaded and listened to offline.

Pop-up A small window that appears over an item (word or picture) on your computer screen to give additional information.

Port A computer socket into which you plug equipment.

PowerPoint Part of Microsoft's Office suite of programs. It allows you to create slideshow presentations.

Processor The main brain of your computer.

Ram Your computer's short-term memory.

Ripping Copying data from a CD or DVD to a computer.

Router A device that routes data between computers and other devices. Routers can connect computers to each other or connect a computer to the internet.

Screen saver The image, or set of images, that appears when your computer is idle for a certain period of time.

Security suite A bundle of security programs to protect your PC.

Social networking A way for people to socialise online, typically via a website, such as Facebook or Bebo.

Software A general term for programs used to operate computers and related devices.

Spam Unsolicited junk email.

Spam filter Software or a system that helps to keep spam out of your email inbox.

Spreadsheet A collection of data arranged in rows and columns. A spreadsheet program lets you manage these electronically.

Spyware Software that secretly installs on your computer and is able to track your internet behaviour and send details to a third party.

System Tray An area on your Windows desktop that displays program icons and alerts you when action is required.

Tagging Process of adding descriptive keywords to a piece of information, such as a photo, video or web page, to aid in the search for it.

Taskbar The bar running across the bottom of your screen, from where you can open programs and access the main Windows functions.

Toolbar A vertical or horizontal onscreen bar that's made up of small images. Click these to perform certain functions.

Trojan A computer virus that disguises itself as an innocent program to entice people to install it. Trojans can allow third parties complete access to your computer remotely.

Upload Process of sending files from your computer to the internet.

USB (Universal Serial Bus) A connection technology that allows you to transfer data easily. USB cables are used to connect devices and are plugged into a USB port on your computer.

USB key See **Memory stick**

Virus A malevolent program that spreads from computer to computer within another program or file.

Voice over Internet Protocol (VoIP) Term used to describe making phone calls over the internet rather than via a standard phone network.

Web browser See **Browser**

Webcam A video camera attached to or integrated into your computer.

Webmail Email accounts accessed through your web browser.

Worm Similar to a virus, except a worm doesn't need to attach itself to a document and can simply spread via the internet.

Index

index

▶ Index

index

index

ABOUT THE CONSULTANT EDITOR TERRIE CHILVERS
Terrie Chilvers is a freelance writer and journalist specialising in computing, technology and games. She lives in London and is a regular contributor to *Which? Computing* magazine.

which?
COMPUTING

HAVING PROBLEMS
WITH YOUR COMPUTER?

A few years ago **Which? Computing** launched an online Helpdesk service.
The team has a combined experience of over forty years and promises
to answer questions within five working days.

To date, the team has answered tens of thousands of queries from readers,
and there's no PC problem they won't tackle.

As a reader of **Computing Made Easy for the Over 50s**,
you can now access this indispensable service absolutely free.

To submit a question for the Helpdesk*, simply go to
www.which.co.uk/computinghelpdesk

Enter your query and, where it asks for a membership number,
simply enter the code that you'll find on the page of 'Useful
websites and forums' in the Troubleshooting chapter.

*This service is only available online